Multiple
PATHS TO
Ministry

Multiple
PATHS TO
Ministry

New Models for
Theological Education

EDITED BY
Lance R. Barker
AND
B. Edmon Martin

THE
PILGRIM
PRESS
Cleveland

Grateful acknowledgment is given for permission to reprint "The Small Church: Radical Reformation and Renewal of Ministry," originally published in the *Anglican Theological Review* 78, no. 4 (Fall 1996).

The Pilgrim Press
700 Prospect Avenue
Cleveland, Ohio 44115-1100
pilgrimpress.com

Printed in the United States of America on acid-free paper

08 07 06 05 04   5 4 3 2 1

Library of Congress Cataloging-in-Publication Data

Multiple paths to ministry : new models for theological education / edited by Lance R. Barker and B. Edmon Martin.
   p. cm.
  Includes bibliographical references and index.
  ISBN 0-8298-1610-0 (pbk. : alk. paper)
  1. Theology – Study and teaching – United States. 2. Protestant churches – Clergy – Training of – United States. 3. Theology – Study and teaching – Canada. 4. Protestant churches – Clergy – Training of – Canada. I. Barker, Lance Richard, 1938- II. Martin, B. Edmon, 1939-
BV4030.M85   2004
230′.071′173 – dc22

2004044438

Contents

Part One
ALTERNATIVE MODELS

Part Two
ISSUES IN FORMATION

Part Three
RE-IMAGINING THE FUTURE

Foreword

For two decades mainline Protestants have watched the so-called "crisis in vocations" in the Roman Catholic Church as if we were merely spectators to a phenomenon that did not really affect us. Solutions have been readily offered: Ordain women. Allow priests to marry. Alter hierarchical orders of ministry ill suited to a more egalitarian American culture. Not surprisingly, Protestant "solutions" to Roman Catholic "problems" have not been readily embraced. Unfortunately, while Protestants have been attending to the stick in their Catholic colleagues' eye, they have been ignoring the log in their own. We who have ordained women, often for decades, who have tended to see marriage as normative for ministers, and who for the most part are decidedly nonhierarchical have discovered that we, too, have our own crisis. Indeed, the crisis may be more broadly ecumenical than we have cared to admit, having more to do with our understanding of the nature of ministry itself, and with our engagement with or submission to the culture, than with questions of ministerial practice and ecclesial custom, or with educational criteria for ordination. Ed Martin and Lance Barker help us explore not only the nature of the crisis, but also the opportunity for renewal such a crisis may offer.

The problem is often identified with the phrase, "not enough." There are not enough students entering seminary. There are not enough young students who can reasonably be expected to serve three, four, or even five decades in active ministry. There are not enough graduates of theological schools interested in parish ministry as their primary call. There are not enough parishes able to pay the salary and benefit package expected of a seminary-trained, "professional" clergy. There is not enough power vested in judicatory leadership to deploy ministers to geographically dispersed or economically distressed communities, be they urban or rural. There is not enough access — geographic or financial — for persons seeking to be theologically equipped in traditional ways for ministry. The essays in this book describe many of these realities. But even if we could address each of these experiences of scarcity — and we must address many of them — the crisis would remain.

Between the lines of what follows, Martin, Barker, and their colleagues point us beyond questions of scarcity to a series of distortions in the American church's understanding of ministry itself:

- congregations that view ministry as something the "paid" does for the "unpaid" or on behalf of them
- congregations that see themselves parochially as independent institutions with both the right and the need to "employ their own minister"
- individuals who see ministry as a profession with a career path involving a successive series of "promotions"
- individuals who view ministry and ordination as a right to be claimed or a privilege to be earned with a degree rather than as a calling to be received and exercised

In their own ways, each of the authors challenges these distortions with a call to catholicity, to the understanding that faithful congregations are far more than independent contractors more or less capable of hiring a staff to do their own ministry, and to a theological conviction about the primacy of baptism over ordination, namely, that ministry belongs to the whole people of God, equipped with diverse and complementary gifts, before it is the prerogative of a few.

As one reads through the various experiences of theological education among the people, it is striking to see how they each provide equipped leaders for the church while at the same time liberate the church from these theological distortions. Congregations and pastors begin to lose a sense of isolation, not just geographically, but also ecclesiologically, discovering what *Baptism, Eucharist, and Ministry*[1] describes as the collegial and communal dimensions of ministry. The laity begin to claim their vocation, not in order to "fill the gaps" caused by a scarcity of the ordained, but as an expression of their own baptismal identity. Thus, while the various initiatives described here may solve challenging practical problems in very pragmatic ways, in the end they are as much about the renewal of the church and its ministry as they are about dealing with a leadership crisis or a clergy shortage.

Nothing here should be read as a dismissal of the ongoing and crucial importance of the theological education that is provided by graduate-level seminaries and university schools of divinity. To do so would be to succumb to an enduring anti-intellectualism prominent in much of American culture. Such a dismissal falls too easily into the trap of pitting alternate models of theological education against each other and the even more sinister valuing of those equipped in one way over those equipped for ministry in another. To denigrate graduate theological schools is also, for mainline Protestantism, to endanger its historic role of prophetically engaging both the culture and the public square in ways that require both a passionate heart and a trained and intellectually articulate mind. Theological education is for the sake of sacramental formation and community service with and among the people of God and their neighbors; it is also for the sake of engaging in a prophetic ministry that is at the heart of God's mission. Those who fear a bifurcation or competition between educational approaches as denominations explore these questions will appreciate the many suggestive ways the authors see both models of theological education complementing one another, as well as Martin and Barker's appeal at the end for creative partnerships and conversations.

The pages that follow do not offer simple solutions to problems or pretend that the changes we are experiencing are not traumatic. These are painful times for pastors, congregations, denominations, and seminaries. The problems each contend with are addressed honestly, and the ways each have contributed to the current crisis are honestly faced. But what is also considered is the hunger in the churches for gifted leadership and for a theologically grounded community engaged in far more than the maintenance of declining chapels, but rather with the expansive mission of God. As a result, readers will put this book down not lamenting what we lack, or placing blame, but hopeful for renewed faithfulness.

JOHN H. THOMAS
General Minister and President
United Church of Christ

Notes

1. *Baptism, Eucharist, and Ministry* is a document resulting from over twenty years of consideration by the Faith and Order Commission of the World Council of Churches. Published in 1982, it has since been studied extensively and has had significant impact on churches' self-understandings and on ecumenical relationships. — Eds.

Preface

The face of ministry has changed as the church and its institutions of theological education have entered a new millennium. Demographic shifts and new cultural realities require innovative strategies for meeting the leadership needs of small churches: rural and urban congregations, financially stressed congregations, start-up ministries, and emergent ethnic faith communities. Even midsize churches question their abilities to sustain staff at continuing or past levels. Each of these situations raise questions of the viability of congregations and of their capacity to organize mission in their communities. What are the choices available to prepare and support theologically informed leadership for vital ministries in these congregations?

This collection of essays emerges from a research project conducted during 1998–2000 and funded by the Lilly Endowment. The research project studied the rapidly growing phenomenon within mainline churches of denominational study programs primarily initiated, designed, and carried out within the bounds of a local or regional judicatory. Such programs provide curricular resources that allow one to complete courses of study that lead, if denominational assessment allows, to some form of authorized ministry: certified, commissioned, licensed, or ordained. The significance of these programs resides in the fact that they are being initiated within those denominations that, in recent history, have almost exclusively defined their authorization for ministry procedures in terms of the master of divinity degree. These judicatory-based programs challenge a singular route for ministry authorization, reflecting a growing demand for the shaping of a variety of ministries for a changing ecclesial landscape.

The idea for the book was inspired by a series of consultations held as a part of the research project. Those consultations identified the need for a literature of informed conversation among those that are developing and directing judicatory programs of study. The consultations also identified the need for a literature that would help to widen the discussion heretofore restricted to seminary and divinity school circles. Authors of the essays were participants in those consultations and were chosen for their particular ability to articulate both local and universal dimensions of this movement in theological education.

The essays challenge current cultural conceptions of preparation and authorization for ministry leadership by suggesting that clericalism and professionalism have obscured the wealth of gifts and assets resident within local communities for empowering ministry. This volume engages the contemporary discussion on the status of the mainline churches and the nature and location of theological education, a discussion taken up in such works as Jackson W. Carroll's *Mainline to the Future,* Donald Miller's *Reinventing American Protestantism,* Joseph C. Hough's and Barbara G. Wheeler's *Beyond Clericalism,* and John Cobb's *Reclaiming the Church.*[1] This book is unique in that it is the only work to engage that discussion from the standpoint of theological education and preparation for ministry occurring outside the academic centers of seminaries and divinity schools. The authors of the essays tell the stories of alternative approaches resulting in healthy, vibrant congregational life. They also raise questions and offer critique of judicatory-based programs and call for closer partnerships among the various theological education venues of the church.

The chapters are organized as follows: an introduction to judicatory-based theological education, six stories of alternative theological education models written by program participants, a look at the history of theological education and issues in formation for ministry, and finally, a consideration of theological and cultural concerns.

Editors Lance Barker and Edmon Martin explicate the nature of the discussion and its issues in an introductory chapter. Janet Silman, former co-director of the Dr. Jessie Saulteaux Resource Center, tells the story of this center founded by the United Church of Canada in the mid-1980s in response to the educational needs of aboriginal peoples. The uniqueness of the learning circle and role of aboriginal elders are key components in this five-year program. Carol Bell, writer and member of a local ministry team, recounts the renewal within both a diocese and local parishes through the Mutual Baptismal Ministry Program of the Diocese of Northern Michigan of the Episcopal Church. Isaac M. McDonald, pastor and former director of a program in Eastern Virginia, contributes a chapter on the role of the Southern Conference Ordination Preparation Education (SCOPE) program of the United Church of Christ. This program is designed intentionally to be an alternative educational path to ordination for African American clergy, many already serving as pastors of congregations. Dick Sales, whose background includes many years in Botswana developing theological education by extension programs, reflects on how Theological Education by Extension (TEE) is applied in the Theology Among the People program of theological instruction sponsored by the Southeast Conference of the United Church of Christ. Bert Affleck, faculty member at Perkins School of Theology and director of the Perkins' Course of Study, outlines the Course of Study program of the United Methodist Church, a program with a long history and a sizable role in preparing local pastors in that denomination. Minka Sprague, a member of the faculty at New York Seminary, outlines the history of a seminary that introduced innovation based on a renewed sense of educational and ecclesial mission into both its curricular design and vision of the theological school.

Glenn Miller, the noted historian of North American theological education, contributes an essay surveying the historical place of judicatory education. Ken McFayden, director of the professional development program at Union Seminary in Virginia, raises important formational questions to be considered with regard to judicatory programs. The essay by Thomas Ray, retired bishop of the Episcopal Diocese of Northern Michigan, is a theological statement on the ministry of all the baptized.[2] The volume editors are the research team of Edmon Martin and Lance Barker, who complete the collection with a cultural critique and assessment.

This book emerged from a project that involved a wide range of participants, which is fully evident from the pages ahead outlining our engagement with judicatory-based theological education. It is appropriate that we name the programs and sites we visited and the sites that were otherwise involved in our research. They include the Commissioned Lay Pastor Program of Holston (Tennessee) Presbytery, Presbyterian Church (USA); the Course of Study: Perkins School of Theology; the Dr. Jessie Saulteaux Resource Centre of the United Church of Canada; the Lay Ministry Program: New York Conference of the United Church of Christ and the Northeast Region, Disciples of Christ; the Mutual Baptism Ministry Program: Diocese of Northern Michigan, the Episcopal Church; the Partners in Ministry Program, Nebraska Synod of the Evangelical Lutheran Church in America; and SCOPE, the Southern Conference of the United Church of Christ. As well we want to recognize the service of the project advisory committee comprising Richard Bruesehoff of the Office of Lay Leadership Support for the ELCA; Michael Dash of the Interdenominational Theological Center; David Esterline of McCormick

Theological Seminary; Judith Hjorth of the Connecticut Conference of the UCC; Ken McFayden of Union Theological Seminary–Presbyterian School of Christian Education; Glenn Miller of Bangor Theological Seminary; Anne Reissner of the Center for Research and Study at Mary-knoll; Doyle Turner of the Indigenous Theological Training Institute; and Marcel Vasquez of La Puerta Abierta United Methodist Church.

We thank the contributors to the volume. In a significant way they are spokespeople for the array of people who not only gave us insights but opened the doors of hospitality to our inquiries about their experiences and commitment to the ministries of the church. In particular we want to thank Carol Bell for her assistance in editing the essays as we constructed the design of this volume.

Finally, these acknowledgments would be incomplete without recognizing the financial support and encouragement of the Lilly Endowment, Inc. We trust our readers will share the same sense of thanksgiving for the insights and stories this book presents.

Notes

1. See Jackson W. Carroll, *Mainline to the Future: Congregations for the 21st Century* (Louisville: Westminster John Knox Press, 2000); Donald E. Miller, *Reinventing American Protestantism: Christianity in the New Millennium* (Berkeley: University of California Press, 1999); Joseph E. Hough and Barbara G. Wheeler, *Beyond Clericalism: The Congregation as a Focus for Theological Education* (Atlanta: Scholars Press, 1988); and John B. Cobb Jr., *Reclaiming the Church* (Louisville: Westminster John Knox Press, 1977). These texts represent a wide range of discussion included in numerous other volumes.

2. At the time of our research, the Internet-based program at the University of Dubuque Theological Seminary designed to prepare commissioned lay pastors was in its initial stages. Had that or other online programs been operating, we would have considered that innovation as part of our research agenda.

Multiple
PATHS TO
Ministry

Introduction

Judicatory-Based Theological Education

LANCE R. BARKER and B. EDMON MARTIN

The following essay provides an overview of the outcomes of a two-year study of judicatory-based theological education. The research was funded by a grant from the Lilly Endowment, Inc. We define judicatory-based theological education as theological study designed and administered primarily by a denominational body. Such programs are geared to prepare persons for some form of authorized ministry whether that be ordination, commissioning, licensure, certification, or some other designation approved in a denomination's polity.

In a number of denominational contexts during the past several years, theological education programs directed toward preparing persons for various forms of authorized ministry have taken on a new prominence. The essays in this volume grows out of an extensive research project and reflect on the background and current relevance of these programs. The problem that initially engaged us was whether these judicatory-based theological education programs existed in sufficient numbers to form a strategic ecclesial and educational mass or movement that by its very existence calls for a reexamination of the ways theological education takes place. We soon discovered a deeper set of issues existing in the ecclesial shifts occurring within the constituencies of the theological schools.

Consequently, this book and the research[1] leading up to it join the considerable discussion raised by a number of authors who have assessed the relation of theological schools to the institutional viability of the mainline churches. The book and research also questioned what constitutes a theologically effective curriculum and explore the culture of the theological school. The discussion about the nature and mission of the theological school led us to explore an approach that opened the door to discuss the wider "system" of theological education. The programs

3

at the core of our research were in the Episcopal Church, the Evangelical Lutheran Church in America, the Presbyterian Church (USA), the United Church of Christ, the United Church of Canada, and the United Methodist Church. A wide range of programs exists in several other denominations and in the contexts of various institutes and study centers; our research, however, centered on the named denominations because of their shared histories in the development of graduate theological education that grants a MDiv (or BD) degree to certify persons for ordination and to deploy them in ministry.[2]

Our study revealed almost two hundred judicatory-based programs among these denominations, with more being developed all the time. The most compelling finding, however, was the extensive group of people being prepared for church leadership through them. Were the programs, alone, agencies for adult lay education, their significance would rest in an effort by the churches to develop a more informed laity. However, we saw these programs reshaping understandings in several denominations of the nature of authorized or ordained leadership and the manner in which that leadership is prepared and deployed. In the words of Rayford Ray, an Episcopal missioner in the Diocese of Northern Michigan, "At first [the founding of a judicatory-based program] is because of remoteness and economic issues — in some cases it is an act of desperation. But within that context people begin to become aware of the possibilities of a new understanding of church."[3]

Our initial survey included 158 different programs in the six denominations of our study, from which we received 104 completed responses. We did not include seminary-based alternative education programs, such as the Indian Ministries Program at United Theological Seminary of the Twin Cities. Our research revealed that the resurgence of interest in alternatives for theological education was a response to contemporary challenges facing both Protestant and Catholic communions. These challenges, though wide-ranging, revolved around membership, funding, and missional crises, finding specific focus in providing authorized pastoral leadership for small congregations, preparing pastors for new ethnic communities, and providing staff for churches. Gene Miller, a UCC Conference minister, speaks for many when he says, "In South Dakota, we are a sparsely populated conference and state. We have around a hundred churches. One-third have around fifty members. Increasingly it is difficult to find ordained clergy to serve those churches. In the foreseeable future, it will not get better. We are in need of pastors.

It [the judicatory-based program] puts a little less stress on the system of finding ordained clergy to serve these churches."

The programs we studied had a distinctly denominational identity based on the ways in which leadership was raised up and defined in each judicatory. At the same time, innovative thinking in ecclesiology, theology, and the practice of ministry relative to their particular contexts informed program character and outcomes. Financial viability, geographic location, and historical or cultural identity were the most often-cited problems or concerns related to program development. In no case did informants look upon their programs as a substitute for graduate theological study. Rather, the stated issue was whether the MDiv should be the only route to some form of authorized ministry and, equally, whether the MDiv could adequately provide contextually relevant and affordable ecclesial leadership for every setting.

Our research included a survey of advanced students and graduates from fifteen of the programs we chose for more in-depth study. About one-half of the students in that sample had some undergraduate or graduate study. A limited number had gone on to attend seminary, but most stayed in their home communities, retaining their own employment positions. Gender makeup varied considerably among programs but overall contained equal numbers of women and men. A majority of students were over fifty years of age, an older student body than is the case in the mainline graduate theological schools. Of those students who did serve churches, most served small congregations. A limited number served as associates or assistants in multistaffed churches or in some form of chaplaincy ministry.

We found that most programs admitted students on the basis of call to ministry, prior service and commitment to the church, and gifts for ministry rather than on academic credentials. A preponderance of persons surveyed was motivated to enter a judicatory-based program through some form of particularized or communal learning or formation event in their congregation. Students were highly motivated. Without exception they expressed a deep commitment (a) to the educational demands placed upon them and (b) to the events, such as retreats or extended courses, that were intended to develop a sense of educational and faith community. One program director summarized what we found to be the general spirit: "We have focused our program on the servanthood motif. People really see it as servanthood. They are ready to serve wherever they are needed."

The majority of graduates said they were moderately to very involved in their local churches prior to beginning their course of study, and most remained active in their home church after completing the program. Upon graduation students tended to serve in part-time or supply positions. One half of the students/graduates had other work from which they earned income. The exception to these figures is those persons who are registered in or who have completed the United Methodist Course of Study. A significant number of those persons are serving as local pastors or engaged in a process that leads to some form of official appointment in an annual conference.

We discovered that programs were inclined toward a model or method consistent with their own theological or ecclesiological rationale, but they also tended to make curricular choices according to what best served their local needs. Generally speaking at least four approaches to curricular structure were used: (1) a defined set of courses, often taken with a cohort of participants; (2) a facilitated process utilizing retreats, workshops, or small group processes, and requiring supervised or mentored independent study following specific guidelines; (3) a process of study using a set of requirements that allows participants to function independently, selecting courses at colleges, seminaries, and graduate schools; (4) a study and formation process based within a local congregation involving a cohort of members called by that congregation to its several ministries. Whatever the design, the outcome of completing the prescribed study combined with a form of denominational assessment qualifies one to be authorized to serve in some form of legitimated ministry.

Regardless of curricular structure, subjects of study were apt to conform to typical seminary patterns. Faculty came from three sources: seminary and college teachers, local pastors, and local or regional experts. Course delivery was inclined to be traditional, using lectures, readings, workshops, and small-group discussions. From what we observed, there was minimal use of distance learning technologies, not because of a lack of interest but because of a lack of availability, accessibility, and relevant resources. Curricular experience seemed to be more closely related to ecclesial practice than is the case in a typical graduate school classroom, perhaps because both students and programs remained contextually proximate to their faith communities.

Our site visits to congregations indicated that preparation for ministry in one of the denominational judicatory programs was often an occasion for congregational revitalization. In more than one situation ministry leadership had been redefined and reconfigured, adding both breadth and depth to the ministries of the congregations involved. Given the situations and needs of their particular contexts, graduates of these programs provided able, even exceptional, ministry leadership. At the same time, we found a longing, in some settings, for a seminary-trained clergyperson, not because of any perceived inadequacy on the part of the lay pastor or commissioned leader, but because of a congregation's own perception of what was normative.

When we began our study of judicatory-based theological education we did not know what we would find. We were not even sure of a descriptive title for what we were investigating and began by calling our project Alternative Theological Education, because it was other-than-seminary theological education. We were not far into our inquiry before realizing that we had grossly underestimated the scope of the phenomenon. Very early we changed our nomenclature to Alternatives *in* Theological Education, reflecting our discovery of both the breadth and significance of these programs in preparing people for leadership in the churches' ministries. We found that theological education among the denominations studied was much more extensive and diverse than usually assumed, taking institutional form in multiple ways and leading to multiple legitimated leadership roles. Even those with responsibility for these programs, for the most part, did not realize the extent of the phenomenon. We concluded our study convinced that these programs are vital components in the theological landscape. They are creatively attending to the leadership needs of congregations that are sometimes considered by themselves and, often, by denominational leaders as on the margins of economic and demographic viability. In many cases, the programs serve to stimulate ecclesial revitalization.

Signs of creativity and renewal were evidenced in a number of observations construed from our research. First, these programs tended to widen access to the resources of theological education, making theological study available to recognized and confirmed church leaders. Education in these programs provided skills, enrichment, and authorization for ministry leadership already "called out" rather than credentials for a future vocation. Continuing education was generally required or at least expected. In the words of retired Episcopal Bishop Tom Ray of Northern Michigan,

> We are attempting to offer not a watered-down seminary curriculum, but a whole different approach. The typical approach

to learning in our culture has been described by some as "front-end loading," whereby there is intensive education before an individual takes up responsibilities. Then one is licensed or otherwise credentialed for ministry... and though there is always hope for continuing education, the norm is that one is considered an "expert."... Our approach is not front-end loading, but lifelong learning. We are hoping to transform congregations into learning communities.... Thus the program is not intended to be an extensive, all-inclusive training program, but almost an orientation to the lifelong task of learning.

Second, these programs were apt to reinforce the contextual and connectional character of ministry, often resulting in ministries of local empowerment in church and community. Graduates were inclined to stay in their home judicatories where they were authorized for particular ministries and where that authorization had to be renewed periodically. Hence, they were less apt than expatriate clergy to understand their ministries as transitional. Typically, they were also more connectionally interrelated with their ecclesial and geographic communities.

A third observation was that churches that were served by graduates of judicatory-based programs time and again exhibited renewed energy and self-worth as a result of being liberated from having to measure their viability in terms of economic or demographic capital. Freed from the stresses produced by a singular model for ministry and ministry preparation, church people were enabled to value who they were and imagine who they might be. For example, the Episcopal Diocese of Northern Michigan has grounded its program in a theology of baptismal ministries, encouraging the discernment and development of each person's ministry within a congregation, while other programs have evolved around theologies of gifts.

Finally, these programs represented more than an expedient response to declining faith communities. They were creating models for a renewed vision of ministry and what it means to be the church. Consequently, these programs should be considered as more than stopgap efforts in the midst of declining membership, resources, and vision. Appreciation for local congregations and their communities, recognition and inclusion of the multitude of gifts of the baptized, and the democratization of theological study are attributes that we witnessed to one degree or another in each of our field visits. These themes contributed to the stabilization and growth of religious capital in areas where geographic, economic, and cultural conditions require new and authentic leadership models. Raymond Hargrove, a UCC associate Conference minister in North Carolina, summarized these conclusions: "I think more and more that these programs are going to become vital. These programs can become complementary components of ministry leadership preparation. They need to be undergirded. Churches deserve competent leadership even though they are unable to afford a seminary-trained person." This comment suggests the need to reconceptualize and develop educational practices that shape a new paradigm of theological education and its role in empowering church leadership and congregational life. We may discern new paradigmatic directions in the contrasting pressures that face the institutional structures of theological education. On the one hand, theological schools engage in energetic recruitment programs to attract students, readjust their educational methods through distance-based and technologically enhanced study programs, serve students older than student bodies of prior generations, and reshape their degrees to resource a wider conceptualization of religious leadership. On the other hand, denominational leaders struggle to provide authorized leaders for congregations often defined by certain distinctive characteristics: small membership, lack of financial capability, ethnic identity, constituencies unable to uproot themselves to attend a theological school, and geographic isolation. The inquiry, then, of the denominational officials to the seminary(ies) as to how theological education is to be adapted to the context outside the school brings together not necessarily competing agendas. These agendas converge at points where both the theological school and denominational requirements face pressing questions. Reinventing or inventing educational structures and pedagogical approaches may be the final outcome of struggling with these questions. The critical issue is understanding what allows any model of theological education to serve the church and its mission.

We ask two focal questions for the purposes of this volume, take two convergent directions. On the one hand we ask, how are we to measure the viability of a congregation and the character and practices of its faith and ministry? On the other hand, what are the ways pastoral and congregational leadership most effectively can be empowered relevant to the contexts within which ministry is exercised? The questions converge at those points where models of substantial and effective theological education are envisioned and institutionalized.

The multifaceted contexts and institutional realities of the contemporary congregation are the foci around which the discussion takes place.

Surely, congregational existence should be understood in terms of the coming together of faithful disciples for mission and ministry — *where two or three are gathered* in Christ's name. There is no numerical value placed on this dimension of viability except that there be more than one member. However, viability is also related to demographic and economic sustainability. Unfortunately many churches across this country, a number related to the old mainline denominations, are engaged in a life-and-death struggle because of population outmigrations and changed or depressed economies. Consequently these denominations find their primary concern for mission and ministry placed in jeopardy. Can sustainability be redefined for those contexts where vital faith communities are caught in the oppressive grip of these threatening geographic, demographic, and economic conditions? What role does the theological education community have to play in providing solutions to preparing effective leadership in the challenged contexts?

If threats incur jeopardy for what has been called the mainstream denominations, new challenges to theological education arise from those ecclesial communities that claim success and growth. In *Reinventing American Protestantism,* Donald E. Miller identifies a cultural and paradigm shift yielding what he calls "new paradigm" congregations.[4] Some represent the old mainline traditions. Others are independent or associate themselves with other similar congregations. Jackson Carroll identifies them as posttraditional congregations.[5] These independent congregations are highly responsive to the lifestyles associated with the generations born after 1945 and emergent in U.S. society since the 1960s. Among the characteristics of these new-paradigm congregations are high reliance on lay leadership, contemporary worship, small-group ministries, and views that seminary training of clergy is optional.

Whether from a position of vulnerability or privileged opportunity or from alternative cultural and ecclesial understandings, several questions may be posed. What models of leadership are called for if such a redefinition of ministry leadership is to occur, and what forms of theological education would be needed to prepare those leaders? These questions are either recognized or lie just below the surface of recent discussions about the character and style of theological education provided by the theological school. Questions about the economic viability, the pedagogical style, and the impacts of cultural change on religious institutions have been the points of stress that have driven seminaries to curriculum revision and to discussions of how to be more relevant to their constituencies.

Movements to strengthen field education and to introduce globalization and cross-cultural requirements, programs in spiritual formation, research into educational practices that yield "readiness for ministry," experiments in distance education, and attempts to address gender and age of students all raise questions about how theological schools are to function. Seminary faculty face added responsibilities, and curricular resources to face the challenges of innovation are spread thin.

We must be clear on this point: Seminary and divinity school education is better at what it does than at any time in its history. Overall, we believe that theological scholarship and the tools of theological study are more finely shaped over a broader spectrum of theological education than ever before. Much creative thinking has gone on in the past twenty years about what constitutes a good master of divinity degree. The doctor of ministry and master of arts curricula have added significantly to the higher theological education capital of the mainline churches. As good as contemporary theological education is, however, it represents a narrowed view of what theological education could and should be. The problem is not with theological education as it exists. It is not with what theological education does and does quite well. The problem resides in the limited scope of theological education and how we think about it. From the contexts of our study and our general experience, we find that there is a wider hunger within many faith communities of the mainline churches for tools of theological reflection that can be applied and utilized in locally authorized ministries. That hunger is held captive to the dominant models of professionalized and bureaucratized ministry shaped by the theological school.[6]

We have come to believe that judicatory-based programs are authentic and important expressions of theological study, preparing persons for various ecclesial ministries. We believe these programs are here to stay for the long haul and that they hold potential for church renewal and for fuller recognition and inclusion of the ministries of all the baptized. We also believe that this conclusion underscores the continuing significance and necessity of the graduate theological school as the theological center of the churches, but with both more extensive and more limited understandings of its role: more extensive in its sense of service to the educational and leadership needs of the churches and more limited in its understanding of what it can provide alone. Denominational judicatory-based programs and regional theological schools, together, present the best possibility for a broader, richer fabric of education for ministry leadership and, consequently, a fuller recognition and use of baptismal gifts.

The research project emerged when the editors of this volume decided to follow a hunch — a hunch that yielded a project that took us into a variety of denominational study programs that prepare persons for various forms of pastoral ministry and into congregations served by these theologically educated leaders. As we explored the emergence of judicatory-based theological programs, we developed a deep conviction that the emergence of these programs was not some sort of competitive movement with seminaries and divinity schools but an authentic expression of the desire to have theological education be more accessible to the full range of people discerning God's call to be in some form or another of authorized ministry.

Notes

1. Our research design, conducted from 1998 through 2000, included these elements: (1) the development of a list of existing judicatory-based programs among several Protestant denominations out of which research targets were selected; (2) a mail and, then, follow-up telephone survey to a select group of program leaders and participants; (3) site visits to participate in an educational event and site visits to congregations served by those who have completed a study program; (4) a survey mail questionnaire to a select group of program graduates; (5) two major consultations of program participants and denominational and seminary leaders to test our findings; and (6) publication of the research.

2. For a comprehensive statement of our research, see Lance R. Barker and B. Edmon Martin, *Alternatives in Theological Education: An Examination of the Characteristics and Outcome of Denominational Judicatory Study Programs Which Prepare Persons for Commissioned, Licensed, Ordained or Otherwise Authorized Ministries* (New Brighton, Minn.: United Theological Seminary of the Twin Cities, 2000).

3. All quotes from individuals consulted in our research are from individual interviews that are recorded in the field notes documenting our research.

4. See Donald E. Miller, *Reinventing American Protestantism: Christianity in the New Millennium* (Berkeley: University of California Press, 1999).

5. See Jackson W. Carroll, *Mainline to the Future: Congregations for the 21st Century* (Louisville: Westminster John Knox Press, 2000).

6. See John B. Cobb Jr., *Reclaiming the Church* (Louisville: Westminster John Knox Press, 1988).

Part One

ALTERNATIVE MODELS

One

Keepers of the Vision

Aboriginal Community-Based Learning for Ministry

JANET SILMAN

This chapter describes the program of the Dr. Jessie Saulteaux Resource Centre, an Aboriginal learning center for Christian ministry located in Canada. I introduce several communities that the Saulteaux Centre students serve and then explore an Aboriginal community-based learning model that emphasizes "life in the learning circle." I conclude by offering some reflections on the Centre's contributions and challenges both to theological education and to the wider church.

Flying north from Winnipeg, the geographical center of Canada, our small plane passes over miles and miles of water, rock, and trees. Below us now lies the rugged Cambrian shield, which is punctuated by gold Tamaracks, deep-green spruce trees, and countless sparkling lakes and rivers. This is the country that hunters and fishers from the United States pay huge fees to visit. But none of us is here because of the terrain or the wildlife. We are here to visit students of theology.

We land at the First Nations[1] community of Island Lake. There to meet our plane are the chief and the tribal council. Quite to our surprise, they ask for our help. They ask us to come with them immediately and speak with the local high school students, many of whom are alienated and acting out in self-destructive ways; some are suicidal.

The three of us are theology teachers and strangers to this community; we wonder how we can be of help. But we agree to the trip because, according to the tradition of our Cree and Ojibway elders, one always says yes if asked for help.

Arriving at the high school, we find a modern building populated by a variety of young people, many of whom are wearing the colors of urban

15

street gangs. Successively, we visit classes, talking with students about respect — the topic that has been chosen by the community elders.

For us, who are visitors, underscored repeatedly is the notion that a massive generation gap exists in this twenty-five-hundred-member reserve.

The elders grew up hunting, fishing, and trapping in a pristine wilderness. The Bible was their only book. To this day, many of them speak little or no English, whereas large numbers of the youth speak only English. Furthermore, by means of watching satellite-dish television programs and video-store movies, young people have come to identify with a global monoculture. They view the world through a corporate-media lens, yet have little or no access to the glamour and material wealth that they see portrayed on television or in the movies. Not surprisingly, confusion and frustration, rage and despair characterize the young people of this First Nations community.

Our visit to the high school leaves us with haunting and disturbing images. We are reminded that students of the Dr. Jessie Saulteaux Resource Centre live and work in a cross-cultural context of struggle, desperation, hope, and crisis. The primary challenge facing the Saulteaux Centre is offering a program of theological education that will equip its students with the tools and inner resources they need in order to serve effectively and faithfully in this most difficult of contexts.

Before recounting how the Saulteaux Centre came to be and how it operates, I would like to take you on one more trip, this time to visit "Dr. Jessie" ministry students who serve in the province of Saskatchewan.

To reach the reserve communities in Saskatchewan, my colleagues and I drive for several hours on straight, flat highway. Then we follow many miles of paved sideroads. Finally, we turn onto the seemingly interminable gravel roads of the reserve. At each of several communities, we spend a day or two with the resident student minister; we talk about that person's ministry, family, and congregation, and also about the wider community. We meet with elders and other members of the church, learning what we can about their concerns, joys, and hopes.

In one community we learn that a congregation's church building has been condemned and must be moved onto a new foundation. The White Bear band council (similar to a town council) has offered to help with the restoration project, but the council's resources are quite limited. Nor are there funds available for the project from the national church (United Church of Canada). The congregation has faced this situation for years. Although the church membership has used other sites for worship services, everyone loves and remains committed to the old church. We meet with the student minister and the congregation, discussing possible strategies for moving forward on the restoration project.

Four hours' drive down the road brings us to the church in File Hills. We join the congregation there as it celebrates the completion of renovations to their building. The membership has worked together to restore the sanctuary, to insulate the remodeled basement hall — even to evict birds from the rafters! This dedicated congregation has had to face many difficulties, including the lack of regular worship services for a period of several years, but through it all they have become a strong, inclusive worshiping community. A sensitive, empowering student minister, who has taken the time to listen to the hopes and needs of the people, has facilitated what amounts to a congregational resurrection.

From File Hills we travel three hours to the city of Regina. There we visit with students involved in "core-area ministries." One such student, Mariah Shepherd, grandmother and respected elder, serves as the Regina Native United Church Outreach Worker. Working from her home, she provides a ministry of presence and advocacy among the First Nations people who live in this urban environment. Many are hospitalized; most struggle with poverty, various forms of addiction, and insidious racism. Mariah's deep spiritual wisdom weaves together the customs and values of both Christian and Aboriginal religious traditions. With humor, sensitivity, and patience, she carries out a ministry that receives little financial support beyond the salary and housing she receives as a student minister.

The second student whom we visit ministers to street people and sex-trade workers. In addition, she supervises an after-school latchkey program for inner-city children. Darlene Shepherd's life experience, including her healing journey as a First Nations woman, helps her work effectively and compassionately with the people she encounters. When we visit a grocery store, numerous people stop Darlene to talk with her and to tell her their news. Walking down the street, we hear neighborhood children greet her in friendship. After spending thirty minutes with this student minister, we can see that she knows her community in depth and has a highly respected place within it.

None of the ministry students we have visited during this journey has chosen to attend a mainstream theological school. Even the few individuals who possess the academic requirements to enter a master of divinity program have chosen "Dr. Jessie," primarily because the program is deeply informed and shaped by Aboriginal values and ways. In addition, many Native people have had extremely negative experiences at white-run schools. Many Saulteaux students have spoken of the emotional scars they carry from their years spent in the residential schools run by church and government. For generations, First Nations children (some as young as five years old) were taken forcibly from family and community. These children spent their early years in the brick dormitories of government boarding schools, far from family and home. Student ministers also relate their negative experiences in white schools, where racism and ignorance about First Nations culture and history were, and are, pervasive. One consequence of such racism has been the fact that, until recently, many First Nations churches were served exclusively by white pastors.

Origins of the Dr. Jessie Saulteaux Resource Centre

The story of the Dr. Jessie Saulteaux Resource Centre (DJSRC) begins in 1984 at Fort Qu'Appelle, Saskatchewan. The Centre was named in honor of an Assiniboine woman who was a highly respected elder both in her community of Carry-the-Kettle Reserve, Saskatchewan, and also in the wider United Church of Canada community. Born in 1912, Jessie Saulteaux was prevented from pursuing her chosen vocation of nursing because she was considered "too dark, too Indian." As a result of this impediment to her dreams, she decided to offer her gifts of leadership at home — in her village and in her church.

In the early 1980s, Jessie Prettyshield Saulteaux was awarded an honorary doctorate by St. Andrews College, Saskatoon. She continued to promote educational opportunities for her people until her death in 1995, exemplifying the quiet strength and deep wisdom of many elders who carry "the twin sacred bundles" of Christian and Native customs and beliefs. The Centre that carries Jessie Saulteaux's name is grounded in the conviction that Christianity and Aboriginal spirituality share a great deal and that they share sacred ground.

Jessie's daughter Bernice Saulteaux was one of the first students at the Centre. She recalls that DJSRC began with one teacher, one room, a few Bibles, and two or three students. In 1987 the Centre moved to Winnipeg, Manitoba, a more central location for students from the northern regions of Manitoba. Since its modest beginnings, the Saulteaux Centre has developed into a remarkable locus of both ministry training and cross-cultural retreats. The campus includes five buildings on thirty-five acres of river parkland.

I began teaching biblical studies at DJSRC in 1989. Of mixed-blood ancestry (English/Cree/Scottish) myself, I chose to minister primarily in First Nations communities. To an extent I am bicultural and, like many mixed-blood people, live between two worlds. During my ten years at the Centre, I taught Bible and, during the latter part of my tenure, served also as codirector. In 1999 I relocated to the west coast of Canada. I continue to teach courses at the Centre, and I remain committed to the life and work of DJSRC students and staff. The picture I hope to offer of the Dr. Jessie Saulteaux Centre and its wider context is from a quite personal perspective.

Origins of Community-Based Theological Education in Canada

In 1980 Aboriginal members of the United Church of Canada (UCC) held their first-ever national gathering. At that seminal meeting, the elders identified education for church leadership as one of their priorities. The elders said they wanted Aboriginal people to be trained as ministers for Aboriginal communities. Previous to 1980, few Aboriginal people had received formal theological education, and almost none of these ever served in First Nations villages. It was, and is, common wisdom that after graduating from university, Aboriginal people "speak another language," and their own people can no longer understand them. At the 1980 gathering, the elders stated clearly that they would not endorse ministry training for Aboriginal church leaders that removed those leaders from their communities for long periods of time. The elders' vision provided both a starting point and a guiding principle for the development of community-based theological training in the United Church of Canada.

Subsequent to the 1980 meeting of United Church elders, two First Nations learning centers were established: the Dr. Jessie Saulteaux Resource Centre, located on the Canadian Prairies, and the Francis Sandy Theological Centre in Southern Ontario.

I would also mention another Canadian initiative in community-based theological education known as the Native Ministry Consortium, which was established in 1985 and which offers an ecumenical master of divinity degree. Native theological students are able to remain in their home communities and take courses at a distance. The Native Ministry Consortium consists of the British Columbia Conference Division of Native Ministries (UCC), the Diocese of Caledonia (Anglican Church of Canada), the Diocese of Alaska (Episcopal Church), and Vancouver School of Theology. Because the Native Ministry Consortium program follows a different educational model from that employed at the Dr. Jessie and Francis Sandy Centres, a description of the Consortium's program would take a separate chapter.

A Culturally Appropriate Community-Based Model for Native Training

Following the 1980 gathering of Aboriginal leaders, and in response to the elders' vision for their people, the United Church formed the National Native Ministry Training Committee (NNMTC). This committee took on the task of developing a model for theological education that would be informed by Aboriginal customs and wisdom, and, at the same time, would meet the UCC's requirements for ordained and diaconal ministry. In 1984 the national church approved the nonresidential model developed by the NNMTC. That same year the Dr. Jessie Saulteaux Resource Centre was founded. Then in 1986 the model received a second incarnation with the establishment of the Francis Sandy Theological Centre.

Although the two schools are free to tailor the model in response to specific regional needs and cultures, both schools must work within certain guidelines. Each has an autonomous board of directors that oversees all aspects of life in the respective organization; most, or all, of the board members are Aboriginal. In the case of the Dr. Jessie Saulteaux Centre, various presbyteries within the All-Native Circle Conference (ANCC) appoint several board members. Consonant with the Centre's ecumenical vision, two board members are recruited from other denominations. Board meetings at DJSRC partake of both European and Aboriginal traditions. Staff and board members meet in a circle, decisions are made by consensus, and traditional ceremonies are practiced. The mood is informal; there is much laughter; there are prayers and sometimes tears; elders always, and occasionally children, take part in the circle. At mealtimes students and staff share news about the far-flung "Dr. Jessie" community, and they reminisce about times and people. Led by an elected executive, the board of directors adheres carefully to the terms of its charter, both as a nonprofit organization and as a theological college of the UCC.

The United Church of Canada authorized the two First Nations schools to educate persons for both ordained and diaconal ministry. The Dr. Jessie Saulteaux and Francis Sandy Centres offer certificates upon completion of the program, but neither grants academic degrees.

The DJSRC board has stated emphatically that the ministry program must remain autonomous, with its primary accountability being to First Nations communities and not to the academic world. The opinion has also been expressed that granting degrees is foreign to Aboriginal culture and traditions. On the other hand, the board has recognized that some students — particularly younger ones — are desirous of pursuing academic degrees, and that academic credentials are useful in the world outside First Nations communities. Furthermore, students who wish to become teachers in First Nations theological schools must, in fact, pursue graduate-level studies beyond the basic ministry program.

In the past few years, the Saulteaux and Francis Sandy Centres have established bachelor's degree programs in cooperation with degree-granting theological colleges. A student of either school must fulfill all the requirements of the basic ministry program and also successfully complete an established number of academic courses.

The joint-degree programs have had a number of positive effects beyond the value that individual graduates might gain. For example, the joint-degree programs have brought recognition and visibility within the academic community to the two Aboriginal schools. Furthermore, Aboriginal students entering these programs have been able to obtain government funding previously unavailable to these students. As relationships between the Aboriginal schools and degree-granting institutions have been strengthened, other joint ventures have come about. Also, the joint degree programs have attracted significant private donations to the Aboriginal schools.

Assumptions That Inform the Model

A number of stated assumptions underlie the community-based model for Native training that the NNMTC developed. These assumptions include:

- Ministry with Aboriginal communities requires culturally specific preparation that differs significantly from preparation for ministry with nonnative communities.

- White racism and the values of the dominant culture have precipitated, and continue to precipitate, social and economic breakdown within many First Nations communities.
- Traditional Native values and spirituality must be recognized and respected.
- Culturally appropriate education must be rooted in the First Nations communities.
- Family and cultural support of the students is essential to the success of the program.
- Community-based learning requires an action-reflection model that involves teachers, students, and community members.
- Although designed to train Aboriginal people for First Nations ministry, the model can also serve to equip persons for service in the wider church.
- The First Nations theological schools are committed to inclusivity — incorporating laypeople and ordered ministers, men and women, adults and children, the disabled and those on the pathway to healing.
- The model is not static, but rather is developing; it will be modified as needed, both to meet the changing needs of students and ministry and also to incorporate new insights into the educational process.

Design of the Program

The community-based learning model comprises a five-year program, during which time students work under supervision in Native ministry settings. Most placements are "paid-accountable" ministry sites, that is, student ministers receive a stipend, although, in special circumstances, students work as volunteers for a specified period of time. Depending on whether or not they are called to diaconal or ordained ministry, students serve in congregations, outreach ministries, social work, or community development. One diaconal student designed his own job description in consultation with DJSRC staff and then persuaded his chief and band council to hire him. (Perhaps more of us in ministry would do well to develop, as did this young man, skills in planning and persuasion!) Most student ministers work on First Nations reserves or in inner-city community ministries; all students are required to serve at least two years in a congregational setting.

Course work consists of forty-five one-week units taken across five years. At the Francis Sandy Centre, students gather monthly for one-week sessions. Given the greater geographical area served by the Dr. Jessie Saulteaux Centre, students there meet in four two-week blocks each year. Students spend an additional week each year participating in the annual Grand Council of the All-Native Circle Conference. During the Grand Council, students assume leadership roles, learning through experience the skills of self-government in the church. Participation at Grand Council takes the place of polity classes in mainstream theological education. Students chair committees, lead worship, write motions, and participate in traditional ceremonies. Often the work begun at Grand Council continues throughout the year; students serve on committees of the ANCC and of the national church.

Normally the elders of a community choose those whom they will send for ministry training at one of the Aboriginal schools. In other words, if the church elders recognize a candidate for ministry, and if that person meets the program's minimal entrance requirements, then the candidate is admitted. The minimum academic requirement for DJSRC is a grade-12 standing or equivalent. Grade-12 equivalency is evaluated on an individual basis, taking into account the candidate's personal maturity — including language fluency and familiarity with the culture and with the traditional ways that are practiced in the place where they will be called to minister. Upgrading of deficient areas can be accomplished during the student's five years in the program. (Such equivalency has been interpreted broadly at DJSRC, taking into account the diversity of cultural and geographical contexts from which students come and in which they will minister.) In the program's early years, many of the students were mature in years; they had been church leaders in their communities for decades. Some were trappers whose experience and wisdom more than compensated for their lack of formal education.

Students must have sufficient reading and writing skills in English to manage class studies and to function effectively in ministry. Because some elders do not speak English, and some young people speak only English, fluency in both languages — Cree or Ojibway and English — is necessary for effective ministry.

The DJSRC governing board always has given priority to the needs of the Aboriginal communities over strict application of academic standards. The challenge, then, for those of us teaching the curriculum, has been to ensure that classes and resources are accessible to people who

often lack highly developed reading skills. I have learned that convey-
ing ideas in simple language is not the same thing as being simplistic.
The better I understand a topic, the more clearly and more simply I
can communicate it. The language of most good biblical resources is
too technical and too complex to be readily accessible for those who
meet in the learning circle. As a teacher of biblical studies, I normally
write twenty or thirty pages of notes as the basis for our studies. Even
though my students learn to use concordances, commentaries, and other
resources for biblical study, I face the ongoing challenge of presenting
course material in accessible language.

Fundamental to the Aboriginal community-based learning model is
the affirmation that learning takes place in two locales: the community in which the student does her ministry between class sessions, and
the DJSRC community that gathers as the learning circle. Community-
based education, then, must take into account both communities and
their cross-fertilization, which accounts for the praxis (action-reflection)
dynamic of the program.

Whereas each school is entrusted with the responsibility of designing
and delivering its own curriculum, the community-based learning model
outlines the areas of study that must be covered. Areas of study are
divided into three categories:

A. *Knowledge* includes the standard subjects of theological education, including biblical studies, church history, and pastoral care — as
well as cultural analysis and study of the spiritual teachings of Native
elders. The theological perspective from which all these areas are approached at the DJSRC can be characterized as a liberationist perspective
that draws on the wisdom of an Aboriginal worldview. Whereas each
teacher at the DJSRC gives his or her subject matter unique emphasis,
we, as a faculty, share a liberation-theology perspective that is rooted
in socioeconomic analysis and in a creation-centered, earth-affirming
spirituality.

B. *Skills* include those needed in congregational ministry — such as
preaching, worship leadership, and counseling — along with community
development and other skills related to leadership in the wider world.
When planning the curriculum at DJSRC, we review skills listed in the
model, taking into account the key question: What do our students need
in order to become effective ministers in their communities? To answer
this question we must listen carefully to a number of voices, including those of the students and the elders. One year, for example, we
increased our focus on ministry with youth and children, because of

the growing crisis among young people in so many Aboriginal communities. Although the model allows considerable latitude, eight weeks per year does not yield an extensive amount of class time. Consequently, curriculum development requires much consultation and a great deal of careful discernment.

C. *Personal Growth and Spiritual Formation* may be the most daunting section for the faculty to design, but here the vision of the elders is truly brought to life. The model explicitly enumerates the spiritual qualities that the program hopes to cultivate in students. These qualities include:

- An understanding of their own spirituality.
- Self-awareness; knowledge of their gifts and limitations.
- The ability to integrate learning with life.
- The ability to perceive God's Spirit at work in individual lives and in community structures.
- A love of heritage combined with an ability to go beyond the past into a creative future.
- The ability to be authentic, self-initiating, disciplined thinkers and lifelong learners.
- The ability to relate to others, to accept others, to exhibit passion and compassion.
- A sense of humor; the ability to face disappointment, to risk failure, and to learn from myriad experiences.
- A sense of solidarity with the poor and oppressed among their own people and also in the global community.
- The ability to minister in a participatory style that will both encourage and support the ministry of other people.
- The ability to care for their own emotional and physical needs.
- The ability to value differences.

The *Knowledge* and *Skills* sections provide, in a sense, the body of the course program, but the *Personal Growth and Spiritual Formation* section most clearly reflects the program's spirit. The program attempts not only to facilitate the gaining of knowledge and skills for ministry, but also to nurture spiritual growth and personal healing. The desired result is a graduate who is a mature, compassionate spiritual leader. Part of the students' growth takes place in the learning circle, and part of it takes place between class sessions, in the ministry and life experience of student ministers while working in their field placements.

In the process of spiritual growth, we at DJSRC see the *vision keeper* as absolutely essential. Drafters of the original education model were uncomfortable with the title "supervisor" because of its hierarchical, industrial connotations. They searched for a term that was culturally appropriate and also conveyed a mutual learning process. They chose "keeper of the vision" or "vision keeper." Each student is assigned a vision keeper — a person who, while performing a supervisory role, also serves as a spiritual and vocational mentor. Preferably vision keepers are Aboriginal; they may be ordered ministers or laypersons. More important than ecclesiastical status is the person's character and intimate knowledge of ministry. A vision keeper knows the joys and sorrows of ministry, is able to keep confidences, offers challenge as well as support, and has time and respect for the student.

A Day in the Life of the Learning Circle

Imagine many acres of parkland nestled in the wide bend of a river. Since 1992, home for the Jessie Saulteaux Resource Centre has been on the banks of the Brokenhead River in southern Manitoba. Over the past decade, learning circles have gathered each year in this natural setting. Student ministers converge upon DJSRC from as far away as Alberta and Northwestern Ontario. Normally a learning circle comprises about twenty people: students, two or three program staff, one or two resource leaders, an elder, and often a guest or two. The circle is open, although guests are limited to persons who are actively engaged in learning for ministry: for example, a theological student from Norway or Japan, or a teacher from another seminary. DJSRC lives by the traditional Aboriginal value that the circle remains open always, but our openness must be balanced by a strong focus on learning for ministry. The staff grants an inquirer's request to participate in course sessions based on what they believe that person will be likely to bring to the circle. No one simply observes; everyone is a learning participant. In 1998, Lance Barker, co-editor of and contributor to this volume, was welcomed as a participant; he joined the learning circle for several days.

Also in keeping with Aboriginal ways, the circle includes an elder, who is free to offer reflections. The elder brings stability, wisdom, and counsel to the circle. On the few occasions when, because of illness or other last-minute emergencies, an elder has not been present, many persons within the circle have commented that the circle felt ungrounded. The experience of the learning circle can be intense; predicting what emotions might rise to the surface is impossible. I recall one elder in particular. Just her presence on the grounds of the DJSRC communicated to staff and students an overwhelming sense of safety. We knew, individually and corporately, that this woman, with her deep wisdom and quiet strength, could handle anything that arose within the learning circle that week.

Some classes are taught by DJSRC faculty members; others by resource people who have been recruited both for their expertise in given fields and for their collegial teaching style. The Centre lives by the principle that all participants are equal. Within the circle all teach and all learn; each person brings wisdom and experience and is to be respected. Everyone shares the responsibility for helping make the circle a safe place. Any personal information disclosed in the circle is to be held in strict confidence. When these values are incarnated, the learning circle becomes a healing circle. Many students have experienced spiritual and/or emotional healing in their lives while they were resident at DJSRC.

Although there is considerable flexibility in the DJSRC curriculum, some elements follow an established pattern. Classes in the first week always begin with a sharing circle. Each person speaks from the heart, sharing stories about what has happened in that person's ministry and life since the last gathering. When one person speaks, everyone else listens. A key teaching in Aboriginal tradition is listening: a deep, attentive listening based on the conviction that everyone has something to offer, an offering from which others can learn. This practice of attentive listening directly contrasts with the intellectual sparring that takes place in many academic environments; in those settings, students seem intent upon formulating a response, rather than upon hearing what another person is saying, much less perceiving what that person is feeling. In the Aboriginal learning circle, conflicting views are welcomed, but personal attacks on another's views are not allowed. The elders teach that if, in the heat of the moment, someone verbally attacks another's views, that person is to apologize to the offended person at the end of the session. I recall that one day a student approached me after class because he felt he had responded with inappropriate anger to something I had said. In my experience at DJSRC, apologies are uncommon, because the injunction against personal attack so seldom is broken.

Although listening fully to each person's story can take a great deal of time, this practice sets the tone for the ensuing two weeks; it is an essential part of what we do at DJSRC. Comprehensive sharing helps everyone to be fully present to the learning experience; community is enhanced; the students see the interconnectedness of their work, life, and study; and the learning circle may be transformed into a healing circle. The sharing circle may or may not be a part of classes again during the two-week session, but we invariably return to the sharing circle at the end of the session.

When Native teachings are the focus of learning, the sharing circle may be used throughout a one-week class. In fact, traditional Aboriginal elders often choose to maintain the circle throughout the class time. When that happens, we truly do experience "Indian time," and the cooks accept the fact that meals may not be "on time."

Our experience teaches us that it is best if there are no more than twenty people in a sharing circle. When student participation has exceeded twenty, the staff has established two sets of classes. But two concurrent learning circles put a strain on staff resources. For the past several years, student numbers have hovered between fifteen and twenty.

Another essential practice at DJSRC is *Integrated Learning,* a teaching method that establishes a rhythm between work done in the full learning circle and work done in small groups. We believe that the learning experience begins with the sharing circle, within which students report on their life and work experience and their discussions with vision keepers and elders. The week's subject matter is presented to the entire learning circle by means of various media — lecture, story, text or notes, role-play, and visuals. Participants then work in small groups, where integration of the material is fostered through reading, discussion, and collaborative projects. Small-group work flows back to the full circle; each group teaches the whole body through lectures, stories, role-plays, skits, or visuals. A student integrates the subject matter into life and work in three ways: through the learning circle, the small-group experience, and also through the process of keeping a journal.

Throughout each one-week class, students are required to keep a daily journal. Program staff receive a copy of each person's journal at the end of the week. These journals help the staff monitor each student's learning, and the journal helps the student connect class learning with ministry experience. There are no exams and few written assignments. Credits are granted based upon evaluation of journals and of class participation. The cycle of Integrated Learning, along with the journal requirement, was developed by the DJSRC program staff through long-term experience with course delivery.

All students, from those just entering the program to those in their final year, sit in the same circle of classes. In this way we put into practice the principle that everyone is both a learner and a teacher. When I began teaching biblical studies at DJSRC, I wondered how this principle could possibly result in effective learning by all participants. My experience, however, is that it definitively does. Whether these methods would work as well in non-Aboriginal settings as they do in Aboriginal settings, I do not know, although I am familiar with cases where it has been tried successfully in European settings, for particular classes. At DJSRC, students who have prior knowledge of a topic expand their understanding without becoming bored. Biblical studies, for example, is such a rich field that we can never exhaust even the introductory material.

In order to give a complete picture of DJSRC, I must emphasize the central place of traditional Aboriginal practices, including the sweat lodge. A dome-shaped structure, the sweat lodge is used for a ritual of purification and renewal, in which participants offer prayers within the hot, steamy darkness inside the lodge. On the grounds of the Centre are both a sweat lodge and a teepee, in which other traditional ceremonies take place.

Students are not required to adopt a particular view of Native spirituality, but it is hoped that, over the course of the five-year program, they will gain a better understanding of their Aboriginal heritage. Students learn how to evaluate both Christian and Aboriginal religious beliefs and traditions, because both can be manipulated for either good or ill. Either Christian or traditional leaders can abuse their spiritual power. Some students enter the ministry program with a deep respect for traditional Aboriginal ways. Others arrive with the assumption that Native spirituality is inherently evil, a point of view they learned from Christian missionaries who taught the superiority of European culture over the indigenous culture, which was characterized as superstitious and idolatrous. Even today this view of indigenous culture continues to be purveyed, causing much confusion and conflict in reserve communities. At DJSRC, culture, personal identity, and ministry are closely interwoven; students come to recognize that, if they are to be agents of healing and wholeness in their communities, they must have pride in who they are as First Nations people.

Contributions and Challenges
to Theological Education

To my knowledge, the uniqueness of the DJSRC ministry program lies in its infusion of traditional Aboriginal values and practices into the essentially Anglo-European enterprise of theological education. The Dr. Jessie Saulteaux Resource Centre has taken a stand that honors the traditional ways of the indigenous people of North America. This stand is based on a conviction that there is much spiritual wisdom in those traditions.

In my experience, many "indigenous" programs, underneath the surface, offer an essentially Anglo-European curriculum (which issues historically from a Greco-Roman worldview). Some Anglo-European-style schools pride themselves on encouraging First Nations people to wear traditional dress and to bring the drum into worship services. However, if the school's accountability remains primarily to "the Academy" — with its formal scholarly standards and accreditation bodies — and to white church governing bodies, then the students, including First Nations people, are receiving education that is formulated by the dominant culture.

As a teacher at the Dr. Jessie Saulteaux Resource Centre, I learned that my academic credentials only had value here if they proved useful to the First Nations students and communities. As a school our primary accountability was, and is, to the communities our student ministers serve. I see this kind of accountability as a challenge to every institution of theological education. To whom is the institution accountable? How is that accountability enacted in the daily delivery of their programs?

Because of my experience at DJSRC, I now see the learning process not as a straight line, but rather as a spiral. When everyone in the circle takes responsibility for being both teacher and learner, the burden of teaching does not fall on one person. Furthermore, the DJSRC model of education helps student ministers learn the skill of facilitating small groups. During my own mainstream theological education in the 1970s, I learned much about the Bible but little about how to facilitate Bible study. In fact, when I was first out of seminary, I discovered that my academic education actually impeded my ability to lead groups of laity. Many of my classmates have said the same. The "lone ranger" method by which we acquired our knowledge of the Bible failed to give us the tools we needed to encourage discussion; we tended, instead, to intimidate laypeople into silence. In contrast, the learning circle experience transfers easily into other settings.

The DJSRC program is designed to give students ample time for reflection on the subject being presented. Class sessions take place each weekday morning, afternoon, and evening; generous breaks and the occasional free evening are built into the schedule. No classes are held on weekends, and students may use that time to visit with family and friends, or to catch up on reading or journaling. The relaxed pace at DJSRC surprises visitors who are from Anglo-European programs of theological education. Partly the pace follows cultural patterns, but also the program was designed intentionally to incorporate a paradigm shift in curriculum delivery.

Generally, over a two-week period, people are able to learn only a limited amount of material, after which learning they become saturated and exhausted. Consequently, when designing a short-term, intensive class experience, one must forego the goal of imparting a wide breadth of material. Although course material may be expanded upon by assignments to be accomplished before and after the class sessions, at DJSRC we cannot hope to cover as much content as could be covered in an academic setting, where students attend several hours of classes weekly over the span of an entire semester. In community-based education, we attempt to provide students with the tools they need to access information themselves, rather than to present them with a comprehensive survey of a given subject. In my own field of biblical studies, for example, I cannot impart to my students the breadth of knowledge I received in a residential program of theological education. My primary teaching goals are to foster in my students a love for biblical studies, and to introduce them to methods by which they may access further information from commentaries, concordances, and other resources.

The Aboriginal community-based learning model has certain fundamental goals: to enable students to think critically, to stimulate their curiosity, and to impart the joy that comes from being lifelong learners. In my experience, classes at DJSRC are fun as well as hard work; the excitement of twenty people learning together is often palpable. I have seen non-Aboriginal community-based programs of theological education overload their intensive courses with material. My concern is that this overloading will produce yet more ministry workaholics.

Persons involved in community-based education often feel pressure to prove that their programs are as valid as their academic counterparts. I submit that a paradigm shift is necessary. We must move our thinking from viewing education in banking terms (depositing knowledge into people's heads) to perceiving education as a means of providing people, particularly adults, with tools they can use in their own ongoing learning. My opinion is that banking-style pedagogy does not help prepare anyone for ministry.

A number of community-based programs in the United Church of Canada have been established that are modeled in part on the Dr. Jessie Saulteaux Resource Centre. Two programs for diaconal and one for ordained ministry share a number of elements with DJSRC. For example, students gather for two- or three-week blocks of time throughout the year and practice ministry between classes. The In-Community Program for Ordination (ICPO) is the first nonresidential model authorized to prepare candidates for ordination in the UCC. Still in an experimental phase, ICPO now includes two groups of students who will be ordained upon completion of the program. These ministry students complete 50 percent of their course work in two-week intensive classes and the other 50 percent at accredited schools of their choosing. DJSRC played a significant role in designing the ICPO governing structure and curriculum; consequently, many components of ICPO are taken from the DJSRC program, including use of the term "vision keeper" instead of "supervisor." DJSRC and the All-Native Circle Conference belong to a consortium that oversees the program, a group of UCC-affiliated theological schools and conferences (regional bodies).

The experience of DJSRC and of similar community-based initiatives is that these programs do an excellent job of preparing men and women for ministry in the church and in the world. Practicing ministry while studying ministry often results in a student's being able to integrate what he is learning in both communities (school and ministry placement). New ideas and skills gained in the classroom are shared with, and challenged by, the faith community in which the student serves. Laypeople in the congregations become part of the circle of learning — and of teaching.

Those of us who design curriculum must meet the challenge of making the courses relevant to our students. By the time they graduate from the programs, they already have spent a number of years in active ministry. When student ministers encounter problems, they can draw on a variety of mentors for guidance and support. Students learn how to work with others, to be team players. And older candidates, who are entering the ministry as a second career, do not have to wait three or more years to begin the work they are called to do.

Community-based programs offer many benefits to the church at large. As congregations age and many decline in both membership and budgets, more and more part-time ministers are needed. Student ministers are able to serve such congregations on a part-time basis. Some congregations, even though they cannot afford to pay even a half-time stipend, have a strong drive to continue as faith communities. In these cases, community-based programming can be adapted to train teams of laypeople. Once prepared, these teams can minister to their faith communities, offering a great deal of the ministry that was formerly provided by a paid pastor. We may be moving closer to Paul's vision that we as Christians possess a rainbow of gifts. "Now there are varieties of gifts, but the same Spirit....To each is given the manifestation of the Spirit for the common good" (1 Cor. 12:4–11). This passage calls the sharing circle to mind in a most powerful way.

Whether it is equipping individuals or laity teams, a community-based theological education program is an excellent vehicle for preparing people who are called to ministry. As denominational funds decrease, there is increasing competition among theological schools and programs for those limited dollars. The reality of church politics, however, is that the most powerful constituencies lobbying for these funds are large, established colleges. Community-based schools and programs tend to be new, less established, and lacking the power to negotiate budget concessions. Most community-based programs operate on a shoestring — or to switch metaphors, on a wing and a prayer. Church governing bodies need to have the courage and foresight to fund generously these community-based initiatives — not only those that serve specific cultural constituencies, but also those designed for mainstream populations. The church's future may depend on it.

Questions for Reflection

1. In the programs of theological education that you are familiar with, what role do culture and cultural difference play? Are students prepared to minister in different contexts? Do the people who are the school's constituency have any input into the shape of the curriculum?

2. What aspects, if any, of the Aboriginal community-based model I have described could you imagine working in your situation?

3. What are the lines of accountability in the theological programs with which you are familiar? Are they accountable to the faith

communities being served? to the academic world and its accreditation bodies? to church governing bodies? To whom do you think these programs should be accountable? In practice, how could this accountability be achieved?

Notes

1. In Canada the terms "Aboriginal" and "First Nations" are used for indigenous peoples in a similar way that "American Indian" and "Native American" are in the United States. Usage of terms varies across Canada. "Native" is occasionally used, although in some contexts it is perceived as having a paternalistic tone. However, the word "Native" is used when we speak of "Native spirituality."

Two

From Survival to Vitality

A Journey into Mutual Ministry

CAROL BELL

In an isolated rural town, a small congregation struggles to survive. The vestry despairs of ever raising enough money to meet expenses. They hope against hope that the furnace doesn't break down this winter. The current minister has rearranged the liturgical space. Some members express resentment that such decisions are invariably imposed from above. The turnover rate for clergy remains high. The period of time between full-time clergy typically has been years, not months. A small church school persists, but little in the way of adult education takes place here. The congregation's relationship to the denomination can be described as remote and disconnected.

Three feet of snow surrounds a small Gothic church building. It's a weekday evening, and the windows overflow with light that warms the blue-shadowed snow. In the basement fellowship hall, men and women of various ages gather around a battered table. Their discussion centers on the role of women in the Bible. One participant raises a question; other participants offer insights. One woman suggests a book that has been helpful to her. The gathering conveys lively engagement, amicable disagreement, honest questioning. No one is identified as the pastor — either by clothing or demeanor. No one person seems to be in charge; decisions are made by consensus.

These two scenes come from the life of the same congregation — Trinity Episcopal Church, Gladstone, Michigan — before and after embarking on a journey called mutual ministry. Trinity and fourteen other Episcopal congregations in the Upper Peninsula of Michigan continue to

35

be involved in a movement that seeks to enact circular leadership, collaborative decision-making, and inclusive, community-based theological education. "When we started on this journey together," says Sue Jamison, elementary school teacher and member of Trinity, Gladstone, "we didn't know where we were going, but we trusted each other. And mutual ministry took us places we would never have gone. Oh, the places you will go!"

In 1982 Thomas K. Ray was elected bishop of the small Episcopal diocese[1] that comprises Michigan's Upper Peninsula. Neither Tom Ray nor the Episcopalians in this rural, remote area could have foreseen what would take place over the next decade and a half.

When Tom Ray arrived, nearly all the Episcopal congregations in the Diocese of Northern Michigan could be characterized as small, isolated, and caught in a survival mentality. Most were not able to celebrate Holy Eucharist every Sunday (the normative practice of the Episcopal Church) because of shortage of funds for support of full-time clergy. Priests in the diocese — all men at that time — were poorly paid, overburdened, and often served several congregations. Many clerics expressed frustration about the unrealistic expectations of the laypeople in their charge.

In partnership with persons both ordained and nonordained, Bishop Ray began to seek ways to break the grip of an ecclesiastical mold that had brought about depression and low self-esteem in both congregations and clergy. A strategy for ministry development resulted and was given the name "mutual ministry." Tom Ray neither invented nor imposed the program; it came about because of the efforts of men and women from one end of the diocese to the other.[2]

How Theological Education Happens in Northern Michigan

At the heart of mutual ministry lies an approach to theological education that emphasizes localized, corporate learning, and that seeks to engage — over a period of time — a majority of the members of the congregation.

Carol Clark describes what happened at her parish, Trinity Church, Gladstone, thirteen years ago: "Along with many other congregations in this diocese, we embarked on a discovery process in which the gifts of every member were identified and affirmed. After that, the vestry called twelve of us to form a Covenant Group that met biweekly for about three years." Members of the Covenant Group are, in fact, usually called to a specific role: priest (presbyter), deacon, preacher, or coordinator of one of the ministries of the congregation. The role of preacher here is not necessarily linked to that of either deacon or priest. Previously in the Episcopal Church, except under special circumstances, those who preached were only the ordained. But, today, in this diocese and under the Covenant Group process plan, nonordained persons often are called to the role of preacher — and not all priests are preachers. Current bishop James R. Kelsey observes, "It seems to be important to identify people for roles and responsibilities relatively early in the process, even though those identifications may change or evolve over the period of preparation." "And in the discovery process," says Sue Jamison of Trinity, "we always looked first at people, not at tasks that needed to be done." A curriculum, written by clergy resident in the diocese, provides the basis of the group's work together. After the course of study (which usually takes two to two-and-a-half years to complete), there follows a group examination. Then the entire group is commissioned as a Ministry Support Team, with some being ordained as either priest or deacon. Nonordained women and men serve as worship coordinators, education coordinators, stewardship coordinators, music coordinators, and the like. In the Diocese of Northern Michigan, the newly commissioned Ministry Support Team does not *provide* ministry, but instead seeks to *support* the ministry of all baptized Christians in the congregation. "We are attempting to shift from the model of one person who delivers ministry to a model of a ministering community in which everyone's gifts are celebrated," says Bishop Kelsey.

When I first encountered mutual ministry, my husband, Martin Bell, was rector (senior pastor) of a moderate-sized congregation in Birmingham, Alabama. He and I were familiar with programs similar to Northern Michigan's that were being developed in the Episcopal Church. What struck us as important and exciting and innovative about Northern Michigan's plan was the inclusion, in the Covenant Groups, of persons not preparing for ordination. Martin has devoted most of his ministry to teaching theology to adults, and both he and I share a deep commitment to the proposition that *all* Christians deserve a first-rate theological education.

In 1995 we were called to the Diocese of Northern Michigan, where, for the next four years, Martin served as a missioner. The word "missioner" refers to a seminary-educated, not necessarily ordained, person, who acts as consultant, friend, advisor, and resource — but never as priest-in-charge.[3] (As mutual ministry develops in Northern Michigan, missioners conceivably might not be required to have completed formal seminary education — if a given individual is deemed to have received an adequate theological education.) Each missioner serves in one of the Diocese of Northern Michigan's four geographical regions. Those churches participating in the Covenant Group process, whether they are in the stage of education or that of Ministry Support Team enactment, rely heavily on missioners for support, resources, and expertise in theology and liturgics. Charlie Piper, a missioner and also rector of Holy Trinity Church, Iron Mountain, comments: "I've tried to follow the principle that the missioner is not the primary teacher. Other than in early sessions [of the Covenant Group], leadership comes from the group itself. At first, there is a tendency for the group to look to me, or another missioner, as the expert. That tendency declines as the members become confident of their own ability to lead. Then I become a participant in the learning session, someone who is a resource in terms of where else to go, what to pursue next." Virginia Peacock, also a missioner, says, "I think I have given people a security and a confidence about what we were doing."

Paths to Ordination in the Episcopal Church

In the Episcopal Church, a postgraduate, three-year seminary education has been normative for ordination to priesthood. However, Episcopal Church law (specifically Title III, Canon 9) also makes provision for ordination of priests who have pursued alternative educational tracks.

Jim Kelsey, present bishop of Northern Michigan, describes the customary path to ordination:

> The normal track usually starts with a person's self-identifying, and then trying to convince everyone around her/him that she/he is truly called. [A candidate for ordination in the Episcopal Church must be sponsored by a congregation and approved by the bishop.] It takes on a personal campaign flavor, which quickly works its way into the educational process. These people (usually) leave their communities and go to an educational setting elsewhere. After several intensive years of formation, education, socializing, and identity-reshaping, the person is credentialed and sent off to a new place to "begin ministry." Curiously, that person is eligible to go anywhere — except back to the community that first identified his or her gifts for ministry!

Also, many dioceses have instituted diocesan formation programs, often called schools of theology. Typically these schools are situated in a central (or occasionally regional) location of the diocese. "The expectation of such programs," Jim Kelsey observes, "is that participants will leave their home congregations and travel to a central spot, enter a learning community that is often highly energetic, but also quite distinct from one's own community back home. This tends to perpetuate the dynamics associated with the seminary track." He continues,

> Reading for orders is also experienced in many dioceses. A candidate who follows this path to ordination must successfully complete a guided reading program under the supervision of a mentor appointed by the bishop. The advantage of this approach is that it usually keeps one grounded in one's own community, and it also sets up a potentially rich relationship with a mentor, who may help the student in a quest that goes well beyond classroom sorts of study. Still, this track emphasizes individual study over community formation, and it certainly perpetuates the idea of reshaping one's identity into that of a cleric who is set apart from (and perhaps above) the rest of one's own community.

In the Diocese of Northern Michigan, theological education takes place primarily in the context of the local community — and it involves as many members of the congregation as possible. Rayford Ray, missioner of the South Central Region of the diocese, says that half of the diocese's twenty-eight congregations are involved in the Covenant Group process, with about 150 people presently participating either in Covenant Groups or Ministry Support Teams. Those 150 people vary widely in age, and they come from all walks of life: teachers, mining engineers, retired executives, homemakers, electricians, judges, and factory workers. "Five congregations are now in their second or third generation," Rayford Ray reports, "by which I mean that these parishes have called a second or third Covenant Group into being." The new group undergoes the same educational process as did the first, often with the active involvement of prior participants. Persons identified as priests or deacons are ordained under the provisions of Title III, Canon 9. In Northern Michigan, locally ordained clergy — priests and deacons — are called to serve only in the congregation that identified them. Priests here function primarily as presiders at Holy Eucharist, seeking to be living icons of the priesthood of all believers. In no way are local priests intended to become the pastor, or cleric-in-charge, of a congregation. Usually a parish will call several presbyters, at least partly to avoid even the appearance of one person's delivering ministry to a passive congregation. Deacons seek to enact the servant ministry of us all; they do not simply participate in outreach efforts, but rather they encourage and empower the entire body of the church to diaconal ministry.

To be sure, our diocese is not alone in forging such alternative, community-based theological education. According to Jim Kelsey, the dioceses of Nevada, Nebraska, Wyoming, Eastern Oregon, Western New York, Ohio, Vermont, and the other three Michigan dioceses, to mention only a few, are pursuing similar programs.

When I asked Jim what makes Northern Michigan unique, he said,

> I guess it's the fact that we're so small, and so totally committed to the approach. We've even restructured our diocesan canons to support it. We only have ten stipended positions (including mine), and only two or three of those positions do not have specific ministry-development responsibilities included in their job descriptions. The whole diocese is divided into regions designed to support ministry development as much as possible. As a matter of policy, the Diocese of Northern Michigan is committed to working with communities, rather than individuals, in preparation for local affirmation. Also, our affirmation weekends fulfill the canonical requirements for postulancy, candidacy, etc., in a way that supports community development rather than individualized formation.

Impact of the Process at the Local Level

Missioner Charlie Piper has served in the Diocese of Northern Michigan for nearly thirty years. He has an aura of quiet, deep wisdom about him — but he is animated and spirited whenever he talks about mutual ministry. I ask for some background about how our diocesan educational process came about. "Early in the evolution of mutual ministry," Charlie says,

> the concept was to provide the educational component on a regional basis. Those identified for roles in a congregation traveled to a centrally located place once a month for a series of one-day sessions (they were all held on Saturdays). The meetings wove together several things; I remember, for example, that I did biblical background and Carol Clark spoke on spirituality. Soon, however, we realized that this was not the way to go. Travel was, of course,

a hassle. But it also seemed unhealthy for people to be drawn out of their congregations. It promoted an "us-and-them" mentality. In that way, really, it was not unlike the dynamic that is set up in the traditional seminary model.

What was known as Phase One gave way to the model that is in place today: a Covenant Group that meets in the home parish (with the guidance of one or two missioners) and that follows a curriculum. The present curriculum encompasses eleven units, which were created for the first Covenant Groups when they began meeting in the late 1980s. "As I recall," Piper says, "It was a case of: 'Is it done yet — for tonight?' We scrambled to get units to the groups. That, in part, accounts for the uneven quality of the material." Marion Luckey, a retired elementary school teacher, adds, "The pages were warm when we received them!"

Marion Luckey's parish is St. John's in Munising, Michigan, a small town located on the shores of Lake Superior. She describes her experience of the educational process as being sometimes quite frustrating.

> Some of it seemed pretty esoteric at the time, until we got a better grasp on it. Often I was looking for more than was there; for others in the group, it was about as much as they could handle. But far more than providing academic preparation, the process built community. I received a better understanding of baptismal ministry, and I think we all gained an appreciation for ordained ministry. I found out how much I didn't know, and I learned to take responsibility for asking questions and finding out more. We discovered we wouldn't be castigated for our ignorance. We would be aided in plugging the holes in our knowledge.

She adds:

> I think the strongest thing I remember from our Covenant Group was the group nature of the final examination before the Commission on Ministry. You were supposed to be familiar with all categories, but also, together with one or two other people, you had to make a presentation on one or two topics. The group interaction skills were more important than the content, really. We worked together to help one another feel competent, to find resources, and to accept responsibility for being contributing members of the group.

When I ask Marion if, at the end of the process, she felt prepared for her role as local priest, with a characteristic candor, she replies, "No, not at all. I didn't feel ready at the end. I didn't have a clue about mechanics." The practical aspects of presiding at Eucharist, Marion remembers, were absorbed over time as she and Virginia Wasmiller, the other locally affirmed priest at St. John's, watched and learned.

"I discovered gifts I didn't know I had," says Bonnie Turner, a locally ordained priest from Grace Church, Menominee. "I feel like I've been made a whole person." Bonnie is enthusiastic, filled with life. She tells of a fellow parishioner who was called to participate in the parish's second-generation Covenant Group: "She said to me at the beginning, 'I don't know if I can do that,' and now that same woman is a deacon and senior warden. We are all empowered by this process." About the educational part, Turner recalls, "At first no one wants to lead. Then, after a while, people get confident and they are not afraid to lead. We realized we didn't have to know it all. Soon some people, on their own, would do research for the next session. It was a real surprise." I ask Bonnie what difference it makes to her that she is ordained under the mutual ministry program, rather than under one of the more traditional programs, such as reading for orders. "The difference is the support. We all work together as a group. If someone calls me on the phone about my performing a wedding, I say that I belong to a Ministry Support Team and I have to discuss it first with the team. Liturgical decisions are made together." She laughs. "A woman who was new to the congregation said to me, 'I don't know what kind of ministry you do here, but I like it.' I told her, 'Hey, we'll tell you about it!'"

Paul Kopera, a member of the Ministry Support Team at All Saints, Newberry, agrees that, for him, the Covenant Group has more to do with "getting together with people and forming a group identity, rather than knowledge I learned." One member of the church's current second-generation group, according to Paul, expresses impatience with the curriculum. "He has been called to be a deacon and he wants to know how to be a deacon. And the Bible, for him, is true word-for-word. I think possibly the curriculum is an eye-opener for this man, at least in terms of what we have discussed so far." Paul's wife, Dottie, one of three locally ordained priests in the Newberry congregation, adds: "A woman in the group asked me, 'Why do I have to be commissioned to be hospitality coordinator?' I said, because you are part of a group, and we are learning how to be together as a group. After being in that group for some time, the woman said, 'Yes, now I understand.'" Dottie further observes that their congregation "has come a long way toward saying yes to mutual ministry. Some see that it makes the church work, but still they want to sit back and just be parishioners. That's okay. And then you have others, like Jane and Mac Freeborn, who walk in and say, 'Can we be a part of it?' They are now in the Covenant Group and they're loving it."

Virginia Peacock, rector of two parishes and a missioner in the north-central region of the diocese, observes: "The real value of the curriculum is that it pushes, allows, encourages, makes possible a deepening connection with one another. And that's a powerful thing. For anything associated with theological education to be sound and valuable, that component is key." She relates that, when she was consulting with Holy Innocents Church, Little Lake, the Covenant Group process "brought together two people who virtually could not be in the same room together. We've gotten very respectful of each other." Ginny has also witnessed in the congregation a growing awareness of what it means to be church. "At one point, a retired psychiatric nurse, who was identified as a deacon, said, 'We've spent enough time on ourselves. Now we have to reach out to the whole community.' She was voicing the vision for the entire congregation — that we *have* to be a diaconal community."

The experience of Holy Innocents highlights the ultimate thrust of mutual ministry — outward, beyond the walls of the church building, into the wider community. The Ministry Support Team of a congregation can empower the entire church family to enter into the exciting adventure of being the Body of Christ. "This wanting to be a servant community," says Peacock, "has been a recognition owned by a whole group of people, and it could not have happened if they were not in this process."

Charlie Piper recalls that four members of the Ministry Support Team at Holy Trinity, Iron Mountain, attended an ecumenical gathering in response to Hurricane Mitch. These four inspired a passion in the congregation that has resulted in a diocesan-wide outreach effort called the Honduras House Project. "I didn't even know about the initial meeting. In the old days, I would have been point person on that — or it wouldn't have happened," Piper says. "Our diaconal ministry coordinator, Gail Baravetto, has spearheaded it, but really she and others have enabled the whole congregation to become involved. Mutual ministry unleashed that response."

Still Building the Airplane

Tom Ray often describes the diocese's ministry development efforts as building an airplane while in flight. "It's definitely an evolving thing," agrees missioner Manuel Padilla. "We're not quite there yet," echoes Patricia Green, an interim missioner.

Efforts to revise the educational curriculum used by Covenant Groups in the Diocese of Northern Michigan began almost as soon as the warm xeroxed pages cooled down, according to Charlie Piper. And not every group has used the curriculum as written. Some congregations have rearranged the units. Trinity Church, Mackinac Island, began their education process with biblical and theological study designed by the group in conjunction with missioner Martin Bell. "In that setting, we did some significant work in biblical theology before ever identifying people for roles," Bell recalls. "Then the group moved into the more formal covenant-group process." Virginia Peacock tells of her experience at Holy Innocents, Little Lake: "We looked at the curriculum and then we rewrote it as we went. One person in our group, Jim Livingston, teaches Bible as literature at Northern Michigan University. What a resource *he* is!"

In my own traveling around the diocese, I have encountered nearly universal agreement that Covenant Groups have been, in the words of Jim Kelsey, "tremendously transformative for the communities that experience the process." Nevertheless, many express the opinion that the present curriculum suffers from unevenness of content, at least partly because of the urgency to produce units for groups that were already underway. Some units are described as esoteric, others as too simple. Charlie Piper comments that when he wrote two units on liturgy, he certainly did not envision the group's having copies of the entire unit. "I included possible answers to questions, which unfortunately became *the* answers." He goes on to observe: "Some have asked, 'Is this a watered-down seminary course?' In some ways it is. Its value, I think, is in giving people familiarity with concepts that can eventually lead them to continue on in their journeys." "It is amazing," Jim Kelsey notes, "that even with commonplace content, the process seems to work to help communities grow confidence and a sense of competence. It also helps a group learn about shared leadership. It establishes rapport with the missioner/consultant." Manuel Padilla adds that he has seen the process "spark a thirst in people to learn more." He affirms the need for groups to reflect, as they go along, on the implications of the study — not just at the end of the process. When working with a Covenant Group, he suggests that each session include a time for reflection on questions such as, "How does what we've studied inform our lives as Christians?"

The type of reflection Manuel mentions has, in fact, been embraced in the latest revision of the Northern Michigan curriculum. Two years ago, a formal curriculum revision committee was formed, and its first efforts have been accepted for field testing at St. Stephen's, Escanaba. Jim Kelsey summarizes: "We have added a much more disciplined and structured input piece to each session, while retaining a section for 'engagement' which is still pretty much self-led, with shared leadership, and a maximum of discussion and participation. Thus, we hope to beef up the content without losing the dynamic that seems to bind the group together and to encourage personal and corporate growth and development."

According to members of the curriculum revision committee, the biblical story now receives major attention. "For example, we envision spending at least a year on the Old Testament," says Marion Luckey. "We are trying to build on the best parts of what we have — and also to address some practical issues." Audio and videotapes have been included as input pieces. "And there also is a shift in group process," adds Patricia Green.

> We are putting more emphasis on the importance of good questions, and on recognizing that there are a variety of answers and a broad spectrum of experiences — and then living with all of that. Also, we're building into the process a quick check-in at the beginning of each session. We can share with one another the big changes in our lives since last time and then incorporate those changes into prayer at the end of the check-in. Also, we ask if there are any leftover questions, or new questions that have come up since our last gathering.

A time of reflection concludes each session. "The ideal is to come to a conclusion during the meeting, rather than in the parking lot or on the phone lines."

The units encourage theological reflection by including questions such as the following: How have you encountered the holy since we last met? So what? What changes are we being asked to make in our lives? What have we learned about being together as the Body of Christ? How do our personal stories intersect with the bigger, corporate, scriptural story of the people of God? Content that focuses on the biblical story, Charlie Piper says, "provides a great jumping-off point for theological reflection."

In the groups she consults with, Patricia Green employs a method that encourages interchange and also stretches beyond the formal process. She posts newsprint that remains from session to session, on which participants write issues, questions, or topics of concern to them. Topics not addressed in the formal work of the group may become the agenda for future educational efforts. On the other hand, if a question is satisfactorily answered, the person who posted it may cross it off the list.

Virginia Peacock points to the curriculum's loose-leaf format as essential — to make possible ongoing revision, as well as the inclusion of fresh resources. "For example, current movies or television shows often have meaty stuff with which to wrestle. We need to be constantly updating that." In the revision process, she adds, the committee has given attention to the different ways in which people learn, including visual, auditory, and kinesthetic. "We use different approaches to enrich the experience and appeal to different people. And we hope it will spiral deeper and deeper. When a group finishes the curriculum, they may think they are done, but in fact they will keep going around and around again. It's like the lectionary that pulls us more and more deeply into the same passages."

I have the sense that no one expects ever to produce "the ultimate curriculum." That would go against the grain of a group of people who have grown accustomed to building airplanes in midair. As Green points out, "We should never be too quick to say, 'Now we have it.' Each group has a piece in the ongoing revision. There should always be room to grow."

Education beyond the Covenant Group

From the beginning of mutual ministry, continuing education has been part of the design. The diocese and the four regions have held workshops for persons sharing responsibilities: preachers, education coordinators, stewardship coordinators. Jim Kelsey comments that "this has happened over the years with varying degrees of regularity and effectiveness. Along those lines, MSTYC (Ministry Support Team Yearly Conference) evolved as an attempt to gather folks from around the diocese for ongoing education." Convened at a Roman Catholic retreat center, this yearly gathering focuses on various topics of interest to persons involved in the Covenant Group process, but attendance is open to the entire diocese. "Conferences led by national figures — Ellen Davis, Martin Bell, Louis Weil,

Gareth Lloyd Jones, Kenneth Leech, and others — as well as satellite downlinks have been most helpful," Kelsey says.

What I have experienced attending diocesan-wide gatherings has been an eagerness to learn and a common life in community that erases lines between parishes or regions. Those in attendance sing and laugh and listen and worship together as though they were a congregation that met weekly — instead of a gathering of women and men of disparate ages, occupations, and educational levels, who live at great distances from one another. Notable for an Episcopal Church gathering is the fact that clergy, whether locally ordained or seminary-educated, do not identify themselves as clergy, either verbally or by wearing clerical collars.

Jim Kelsey sees great possibilities for enhancing continuing education in the coming years: "We are really eager to develop a year-round rhythm of ongoing educational opportunities, including the types of things that we already have. I'd love to see us as a learning community, in which there are regular and ongoing learning opportunities of all sorts and at various levels of learning. I'd love to see it all evolve so that theological education engages everyone in every congregation — not just those who are in Covenant Groups."

Recently, Northern Michigan has been designated a pilot diocese for the national Episcopal Church's efforts to structure continuing education requirements for all ordained persons. Kelsey says, "We wanted to participate in this to be sure that whatever guidelines are developed on the national level will be appropriate for our setting — and to our efforts to educate not just clerics, but entire communities, for ministry." Rayford Ray, missioner of the South Central Region of the diocese, serves as director of this pilot project. "We are participating because of our commitment to ongoing learning for faith communities. It is our hope that, within a year, all Ministry Support Teams and Covenant Groups will be participating in continuing education as part of their life and mission. These offerings will come from independent study, congregational workshops, regional and diocesan workshops, and partnerships with seminaries and universities."

Many people in the diocese echo Jim Kelsey's vision. They express a real thirst for more educational opportunities. Marion Luckey says, "I would like to see all congregations, large and small, commit themselves to Christian study, as a discipline, as a group." "If we're to be serious about this path we have started," Charlie Piper adds, "we need to provide opportunities to gather for theological education."

Living in the Tension between Past and Future

To be sure, Northern Michigan's approach to ministry faces prodigious challenges. Not surprisingly, within congregations engaged in the Covenant Group process, not all members have accepted the changes happily. Manuel Padilla states the question that must be dealt with over and over again in this diocese: "How do we respond to the needs of those who are not where we are and still move ahead into the world?" Furthermore, there exists the challenge of reaching persons of differing educational backgrounds. For some participants, the content of any curriculum can be perceived as unsettling, difficult, or overly academic. Some folks focus on tactics, wondering, "When am I going to learn what I need to know to do what I am going to do?" For others, an educational approach that involves theological reflection and shared leadership does not come easily. Patricia Green compares the educational experience here to that of adults entering a Montessori school. "It's a whole new model of education."

As one would expect, numerous land mines lie along the path of mutual ministry. During my years in the diocese I have witnessed instances of opposition to *any* learning process, the avoidance of change, resistance to accepting a call to active ministry within the congregation, and withdrawal on the part of those who had self-selected for a role and were not called to the Covenant Group. Green also mentions two hazards awaiting an already commissioned and established Ministry Support Team: That the nuts and bolts of ministry tasks can consume the team's meetings with no time left for ongoing theological reflection, and that the team takes on all the tasks of ministry, rather than asking at every point, How are we supporting the ministry of the entire congregation in this area?

Slipping back into what is here referred to as "the old model" (that is, the paradigm of one full-time, stipendiary priest serving one congregation) will always be the path of least resistance.

Tragically, erasing distinctions between ordained and nonordained (the word "laity" is rarely, if ever, used) and putting a high value on community-based education can also lead to both unconscious and conscious devaluation of formal seminary education. "In our effort to do new and difficult things and to reject hierarchy, there is a danger in our grossly undervaluing seminary education," Virginia Peacock observes. A new "us-them" dynamic can supplant the former one: mutual-ministry congregations versus those who follow the old model. The diocese has spoken to this latter issue by calling together a diocesan Ministry Development Support Team, whose mission is to explore many options for ministry development — not just the Covenant Group process.

Disagreement over theology and practice and approach and application forms a part of the natural rhythm of life here. For me, it is a telling thing that it *is* a part of life here. Never have I experienced a diocese where hard, uncomfortable questions are raised so often and so openly. "We're not quite there yet" sets the tone of most gatherings. There seems to be acknowledgment that there are no easy solutions. A major shift in paradigm calls us to live in tension between past and future.

We Are All Theologians

Many Episcopalians in Northern Michigan express deep passion about theological education and about the importance of including the entire community in that education. "If it doesn't stretch us, and constantly urge us to push for more about who we are as church, then we have failed," Peacock says. "Quite simply, we can't survive without theological education. And I think to have the whole community involved in the study enriches the fabric and network of who the community is." Patricia Green: "I grieve that most of us have a second-grade education in theology and Scripture. Most people have a capacity to learn about these things. If we reserve this education for the ordained, we continue to hold theological reflection hostage.... Without including everyone, I wouldn't have any passion for it." "Here we are not just going through the hoops to get people ordained," Charlie Piper says. "Inclusion is a part of theological education. Every ministry is given the same honor, the same dignity as every other."

Even the ordination in 1999 of Jim Kelsey as bishop took place in a theological context. The event was preceded by a two-day conference. The first day featured Martin Bell's no-holds-barred presentation on the subversiveness of the gospel: "Everyone who is the church needs to be shoved up against the world's conventions, and then impelled, driven, into the struggle between the deathly powers of the world and the life-giving power of Yahweh." On the second day, persons who had traveled from across the country heard from women and men across the diocese who told of their struggle with diminishing numbers and diminishing funds — a struggle that has given birth to renewed ministry and outreach in the communities of upper Michigan.

Where do mutual ministry and the Episcopalians of Northern Michigan go from here? Headlong into the struggle to determine who we are as church! We continue asking questions like the one articulated by Patricia Green: "How do we keep jazzed and spicy and open and a little bit off balance?" Manuel Padilla urges that we move on to explore, "How can we be a Christian witness in this community, given our resources?" "It doesn't matter what our ecclesiology is," Bell says. "In the end, we are all theologians; we all struggle with life-and-death stuff. And, of course, we never get it right." "We wanted to fight survival mentality," says Virginia Peacock. "We've done that and more than that. Now we want to thrive."

Sue Jamison of Trinity Church, Gladstone, says:

Mutual ministry has been so life-giving for our church. It has opened communication among people. We can state opinions and know we will listen to each other. We know we can work it out. We are deciding our own future as a church community — and everyone has a voice in that decision. When we started on this journey together, we didn't know where we were going, but we trusted each other. And mutual ministry took us places we would never have gone. Oh, the places you will go!

Notes

1. A diocese represents a geographical area, the basic unit of administration in the Episcopal Church. One bishop serves both as chief sacramental officer and chief administrator of the diocese. Other bishops in the diocese, if any, have assisting roles.

2. Tom Ray's article, "The Small Church: Radical Reformation and Renewal of Ministry," in this volume further details the insights that gave rise to mutual ministry.

3. The term "missioner" is used in other dioceses in the Episcopal Church, and it carries roughly the same meaning as it does in Northern Michigan.

Three

Called

An Alternative Path to Ordination

ISAAC MCDONALD

This is a very exciting time in the life of all church denominations as they examine myriad possibilities for future growth and as they struggle with perplexing questions regarding how their leaders are prepared for ministry. Recently, many new expectations have come upon the church and its ordained leadership — expectations levied by parishioners, communities, and the ever-changing world in which the church has its life. Many of the challenges raised by our present historical situation are especially apparent in the life of United Church of Christ African American churches in the states of North Carolina and Virginia. In the chapter that follows, I hope to shed light on one specific program that is attempting to speak to some of the questions that are being raised regarding how the church prepares its ministers. The program is called SCOPE — an acronym for Southern Conference Ordination Preparation Education.

I cannot recall the exact moment or day when I became an advocate for African American clergy who perceive a call to ministry, but who are effectively barred from ordination by denominational church processes. What I do know is that I have long recognized that these men and women have received a genuine call — a call from God.

In the 1980s, several of us clergy within the Southern Conference of the United Church of Christ responded to the very real need of such persons for an alternative path to ordination. What we created was a program that has come to be known as SCOPE. I served as director of SCOPE in Virginia, and continue to serve as pastor of Wesley Grove United Church of Christ, Newport News.

51

SCOPE (Southern Conference Ordination Preparation Education)

SCOPE is not a lay ministry program. Rather SCOPE is intentionally designed as an alternative path to ordination — that is, alternative to the three-year residential seminary route. The program is structured to meet the needs of a set of congregations whose commonality has more to do with cultural and historical factors than with demographics. The congregations served by this program represent the Afro-Christian tradition of the Christian churches founded by James O'Kelly. Many of these churches have their origin in brush arbor meetings that were organized in the years immediately following the Civil War. These churches became a part of the Congregational Christian merger in 1931; the merged congregations entered into the United Church of Christ in 1957.

By and large, the African American churches of the Southern Conference began as rural congregations that were established across the tobacco and cotton belt of eastern North Carolina and Virginia. Many of these same congregations now face the double challenge of encroaching urbanization and rural population decline. Traditionally the churches served by SCOPE have mentored and called pastoral leaders from within their own communities, based on the recognition and demonstration of pastoral gifts.

SCOPE students, for the most part, serve as pastors of congregations; some of them have served in this capacity for a considerable length of time prior to entering the SCOPE program. For these men and women, SCOPE provides an opportunity to enhance both knowledge and skills. I believe that their stories provide an entrée into the context that gave rise to the SCOPE program. Perhaps the following stories can thicken our understanding of that context.

William Carr, a graduate of SCOPE, has served as the pastor of Arches Grove UCC in Burlington, North Carolina, for five years. A semirural church, Arches Grove draws its membership from the communities of Graham and Burlington. Average Sunday attendance is about a hundred persons. In 1875 a man named Archer organized the congregation in a brush arbor located near the current building — hence the name Arches Grove.

During the pastorate previous to Carr's, the church underwent a split. The congregation called Carr because of his demonstrated skill in reconciliation and healing. Prior to Arches Grove, he had served three other congregations, each of which had been in crisis when he was called as pastor. Carr contends that his experience as a deacon in his home church provided him with good models for working with churches in conflict. In that congregation, a small Afro-Christian Church in the "Old Lincoln Conference," his father had also served as a deacon. From the age of sixteen, William Carr was profoundly involved in the life of the conference, always in attendance at annual conference meetings. At age sixteen he was elected superintendent of the Sunday School, and at twenty-one he was named to the diaconate. In the summer of 1971 he was called to be pastor of Bishops Temple, a church of forty members that later had to relocate because of urban redevelopment. Carr served twenty-four years at his next pastorate, Emmanuel Church, originally a white congregation that, after a period of transition, became a black church.

In 1983, while serving at Emmanuel, Carr entered the second class of the SCOPE program. He received his certificate of completion in 1988 and was ordained the same year. Until 1988 the Eastern North Carolina Association of the Southern Conference licensed him as a local minister. "Nobody knew I wasn't ordained," he says. "I served on every committee [in the conference and association] because they needed one of us." When asked why he enrolled in SCOPE since evidently he had enjoyed a full and effective ministry without formal credentials, Carr responded:

> I felt a need. It's like anything else. You have to keep up to date. In life you never get to a point where you've got it made. The world is constantly changing and we need to continually grow; God called us to minister to the changing world, and you can't minister to people if you don't [keep up]. SCOPE helped me reflect theologically. It asked of me, where does this fit into your faith? Maybe you don't agree with everything [in your study], but you understand the logic of it. The church is not stationary. People are the church.

Ricky Allen, the pastor of Hickory Grove United Church of Christ in Raleigh, North Carolina, has completed about half the SCOPE program. Originally a rural church, Hickory Grove has been profoundly affected by urban sprawl. Allen describes it as a family-type congregation with about fifty active members; the church has remained about the same size for a number of years. Their ministers have been bivocational. Allen, for example, owns a printing business. Describing his call to the ministry, he says, "I felt like God was giving me a sermon. I talked with my pastor, and he said that often God calls people into ministry in this way. I tried to resist the call, but once I decided to be obedient to the voice of God, things began to change [for me]."

Veola Johnson, too, recalls a period of time during which she resisted the call to ministry. In 1986 she enrolled in SCOPE, completing the program in 1995. Johnson says that, for as long as she can remember, she has been an active church member, particularly in music ministry and as a Sunday school teacher. In 1991 she became assistant pastor of Union Grove UCC; two years later, when the senior pastor left, she was called to succeed him.

Union Grove is located in an urban community in Henderson, North Carolina. The church, founded in 1978, has about fifty active members. Currently the congregation meets in a converted house, but they plan to build a church soon. Summing up her vision for the church, Johnson says: "We want to see ourselves as more than just a haven, but as contributing to the community. We want to have a daycare for children and for the elderly. We want to do things for families. We also want to start a tutorial program. We are already part of a group that feeds people in the area — we contribute money and food. We are looking for spiritual growth and growth in numbers. We worship once a week and have a prayer service. We plan to add a Wednesday night worship once a month."

Without exception, the clergy who have participated in SCOPE believe that theirs is a Bible-based call. They have raised serious questions that challenge the church's presuppositions regarding ministerial preparation, questions such as: What lies at the heart of the call to preach? What is the source of a preacher's authority?

In order to convey fully the role of SCOPE within the African American churches, I would like to offer a brief review of the history of black preaching and the theology out of which black preaching has evolved.

The Black Preacher

> The spirit of the Lord is upon me, because he has anointed me to preach the good news to the poor. He has sent me to proclaim release to the captives and recovering of sight to the blind, to set at liberty those who are oppressed. (Luke 4:18, RSV)

Every preacher likes to believe that he or she is a great one called by the Almighty to an incomparable task. And perhaps she or he is, for God does not count greatness in the same way that human beings do. But all preaching and all preachers are not the same. I submit that America's black preacher has been, and continues to be, unique.

Rather than attempting to examine the forces that shaped the black preacher, I will simply say that he or she loves preaching. It is a joy to one's soul. Without reservation, both critically and sympathetically, one laughs at the exhortation of one's peers. If it's shouting time, one shouts with one's brother, or weeps in exhilaration in the experience of the joy of the gospel. Black theology causes that to happen uncontrollably.

Black preachers enjoy God's Word. The story is told that two preachers staged a contest to see who could "shout" the congregation the most. The winner "shouted" this intellectual audience by whooping sweet words about soul food: "chitlins, cornbread, black-eyed peas." It was not what he said, but how he said it. The folks loved it.

Whether this story is fact or fable matters little, because the truth is that black preaching lies at the center of black worship; black preaching opens the door to God and to the preacher's theology about God.

Black preachers in America have always had a visible, viable, and potent influence on their people and on society in general. They have been loved, hated, lynched, and even worshiped at times. Few people have been successful in declaring them nonexistent. More than other black leaders, preachers have held in their hands the destiny of their people. Preachers could lead the people either through rugged, encompassing wilderness to the Promised Land, or in retreat, away from the Red Sea and into Egypt's bondage.

Even the greatest black preachers, such as Mordecai Johnson, Vernon Johnson, Howard Thurman, and the black Moses, Martin Luther King Jr., have been open to severe criticism and distrust. Certain blacks have been fearful that even these great preachers, with their eloquence, might lead the race in the wrong direction. Today the same is true. Part of that fearfulness stems from an old saying among black church folks about being made to feel good:

"Honey, did you go to church today?"
"Yes, and the sermon was good."
"What did the preacher say?"
"Honey, I don't know, but it was the way he said it that counts!"

A Historical Review of African American Preaching:
The Storyteller Tradition

Historically, the tradition of African American preaching reaches back to the black storytellers who, in their fables, would talk (preach) in an animated fashion, dramatically using their voices and bodies to represent the subjects of their storytelling. According to Lawrence W. Levine in his chapter entitled "The Meaning of Slave Tales," "Nothing it seems was too difficult for these storytellers to represent: the chanting sermon of a black preacher and the response of his entire congregation, the sounds of a railway engine, the cries of farmyard animals, the eerie moans of spectral beings....In addition, black storytellers would frequently supplement the rhythm and meter of their voices by utilizing bodily rhythm to dramatize their stories."[1] All these elements were integral to black tales. The African American system of oral communication has always been rich in the use of metaphor, analogy, imagery, and a mixture of sacred and secular concerns, including an inherited intimacy with biblical heroes, particularly from the Old Testament. Some have thought that this tradition is threatened by the increasing level of education attained by African Americans, and that these highly educated African Americans will, presumably, expect sermons that contain less traditional storytelling. Nevertheless, the tradition of storytelling is increasingly the topic of serious students of African American history.

In his essay "Perspectives for a Study of Afro-American Religion in the United States," Charles H. Long writes:

> This is one of the cycles of the Brer Rabbit stories. Brer Rabbit, Brer Fox, and Brer Wolf were experiencing a season of drought. They met to decide the proper action to take. It was decided that they should dig a well so that they would have a plenteous supply of water. Brer Rabbit said that he thought this was a very good plan, although he did not wish to participate in the digging of the well because he said that he arose early in the morning and drank the dew from the grass, and thus did not wish to participate in the arduous task of digging. Brer Fox and Brer Wolf proceeded with their task and completed the digging of the deep well. After the well was dug, Brer Rabbit arose early each morning and went to the well and drank his fill, pretending all the time that he was drinking the morning dew. After a while, Brer Fox and Brer Wolf became suspicious of Brer Rabbit and set about to spy upon him. Sure enough, they caught him one morning drinking from their well. They subjected him to some punishment, which we need not go into.

Brer Rabbit is not simply lazy and clever; it is clear that he feels he has something wise to do — that life cannot be dealt with in

purely conventional terms and committee meetings. In many re-
spects, the preacher in the black community exhibits many of the
traits of Brer Rabbit, and it was often the preacher who kept alive
the possibility for another life, or who protested and affirmed by
doing nothing.[2]

Black folklore not only spoke of Brer Rabbit's wisdom, but it also established a distinction between *taking* and *stealing* in the understanding
of slaves. Slaves could both challenge the moral code of their masters
and also have their own functioning moral code, which they deemed
to be of a higher order than that of their masters. Most important to
them were their own vocabulary, their own experience, their own biblical interpretation. Thus they told tales in their own language. And
even without formal training, black preachers connected the tales with
Scripture. Folk tales helped the people identify who they were as a
community. Stories and the storytelling style were key in developing
communal relationships.[3]

If one were to trace the entire historical development of the black
preacher, various forms and styles would be readily identified, among
them the narrators, biblical hero storytellers, and the exhorters. The
latter, it seemed, had authorization to give testimony or lead prayers at
selected meetings, and occasionally exhorters could perform marriages
and preach (although not usually "the sermon" for the day). Some were
self-appointed and some appointed by the community as a part of the
community. The black communal system had the power to authorize
these exhorters — and often did.

To become a credentialed preacher, on the other hand, one generally
needed to be licensed, or even ordained, by an association body. The
Lexington Presbytery, for example, ordained John Chavis as early as
1799. Ordained preachers were allowed to deliver the sermon and also
to administer the sacraments of baptism and communion. However, ordination did not have to be granted by an ecclesiastical body; it could
also come as a result of appointment by a slave owner. Alternatively,
persons in a particular group could recognize someone as having a gift
and "draft" that person into preaching. Even when an ecclesiastical body
gave formal authorization, this authorization did not guarantee that a
black preacher's status would be universally recognized.

In the early 1800s, the systems of authority within white Protestant
denominations discouraged formal education for blacks. In many states,
blacks were prohibited by law from achieving literacy. However, many

blacks became very literate, relying on an informal support system in which people both read aloud to one another at every opportunity and also passed on to each other any learning they had accumulated. On the other hand, blacks frequently dismissed formal education; many black preachers asserted that education did more harm than good.

Preachers — and exhorters who had courage enough to preach — risked danger from slave owners and other white people. Therefore, within their communities, these preachers were often regarded as having more-than-usual divinely inspired authorization. Furthermore, general forgiveness was granted to any black preacher who was required to mimic the slave master or to say only what the master told him to say. In fact, the element of danger may have enhanced the ability of black preachers to function effectively in oral and dramatic ways, and the drama surrounding such preaching may have helped bestow additional acknowledgment and authorization to black preachers in the eyes of their people.

The educational growth of the black preacher was, of course, impeded by the fact that Negro slaves were kept as far from education as possible. However, only formal education was affected. The informal, "invisible" training that black preachers received derived from a system that was shared only by those preachers. This informal system trained prospective clergy in ways that the congregation and senior pastors deemed necessary and sufficient. For example, the training included special assigned tasks and job descriptions, such as youth minister, minister of visitation, and worship leader.

In his autobiography, Frederick Douglass gives an example of how educational systems worked among African Americans:

> At our second meeting, I learned there were some objections to the existence of our school, and surely enough, we had scarcely got to work — good work, simply teaching a few colored children how to read the gospel of the Son of God — when in rushed a mob, headed by two class-leaders, Mr. Wright Fairbanks and Mr. Garrison West and with them, Master Thomas. They were armed with sticks and other missiles and drove us off, commanding us never again to meet for such a purpose. One of this pious crew told me that as for me, I wanted to be another Nat Turner, and that, if I did not look out, I should get as many balls in me as Nat did into him. Thus ended the Sabbath-school, and the reader will not be surprised that this conduct, on the part of class-leaders and professedly holy men, did

not serve to strengthen my religious convictions. The cloud over my St. Michael's home grew heavier and blacker than ever.[4]

Sometimes my clergy colleagues with ethnic and racial backgrounds other than African American have difficulty understanding the relationship between black theology and African American preaching styles. "The Message of Black Theology," a paper prepared by the National Conference of the Black Theology Project, gives this explanation:

> We speak from the perspective we call Black Theology. Black — because our enslaved foreparents appropriated the Christian Gospel and articulated its relevance to our freedom struggle with incisive accents that Black women and men have sounded ever since. Theology because human life and history begin with God, who works in the person of Jesus Christ for liberation from "God-talk" that reflects the black Christian experience of God's action and our grateful response. Black Theology is formulated from our reading the Bible as we experience our suffering as a people. Black Theology moves between our church and our community; the church proclaims the message and the message reverberates back upon the church, enhanced by the religious consciousness of black people, including those who stand outside of the institutional church but are not beyond God's grace and his revelation.
>
> The God of Moses and Joshua, of sister Ruth and brother Amos, of our African ancestors and our slave forebears, had revealed himself in Jesus Christ, the Black Messiah. He has heard the cry of our people, captive to the racist structures of this land, and is come to deliver us as he came to Israel of old in Egypt-land. In our day, the blackness of Jesus is a religious symbol of oppression and deliverance from oppression; of his struggle and a victory over principalities, powers and wickedness in the high places of this age.[5]

Historical Background of the Southern Conference

Any consideration of the black churches currently within the bounds of the Southern Conference of the United Church of Christ must include a historical perspective. I would hope to illuminate some of the factors that have contributed to, and still contribute to, prevailing attitudes in the Southern Conference with regard to ministerial education.

The Convention of the South that later merged into the Southern Conference UCC included many constituencies. Notable among these constituencies were two groups that I will designate as the black Congregationalists and the Afro-Christians. Simply stated, black Congregationalists related to the Congregationalists who originated in New England. Afro-Christians were influenced by the Christian Church that developed out of James O'Kelly's separation from the Methodist Church.

Differences between the two groups stem from several factors:

1. There was a significant difference between the organizational capabilities of the American Missionary Association (Congregational) and those of the white Christian churches. Traditionally the white church had been a very loosely knit denominational fellowship, whose constituent churches were not always known for a strong or unified sense of identity. The American Missionary Association, by comparison, responded to perceived mission needs with the strength and support of what was basically New England Congregationalism.

2. The white Southern Christian Church exhibited a racial bias generally absent from the Northern white mission perspectives of New England Congregationalism. There is no doubt that some white leaders — particularly pastors — were genuinely concerned with helping freed black folk establish their own churches. Nevertheless, there can also be no doubt that black folk received little support, either financially or morally, from white churches. Not much else could be expected in a culture where, by and large, black men and women had been regarded as property. Northern mission activities did not have to contend with as much racism as did the southern efforts. Efforts in New England to raise funds and other forms of support met with reasonably good success. Even though genuine and vigorously pursued, efforts undertaken by the northern Christian Church had to contend with southern white racism.

3. Following the Civil War, those in the South willing to assist in the development of black churches found themselves seriously hampered by the South's unhappy economic situation. It is difficult to comprehend fully the war's disastrous impact on the southern states — not just financially, but also emotionally and regarding cultural self-esteem. Southern society was beaten, drained, ravaged, and downtrodden. There was little incentive to be "mission minded." The need for reconstruction was so great that little energy or motivation remained for consideration of black people's needs.

4. There was a difference between the Afro-Christians and black Congregationalists with regard to initiating the establishment of black churches and educational institutions. Available records seem to suggest

that in the case of Afro-Christians, the initiative for improvement of religious and educational conditions came from within their own group; these initiatives were then responded to by others in the area associated with the white Christian Church. For those who became black Congregationalists, the initiative seems to have come, in large measure, from the American Missionary Association (A.M.A.) and from the New England Congregationalists who became aware of the plight of southern black people.

There is a commonly held misconception that only black Congregationalists received education in any substantive way — and that through the work of the A.M.A. The fact is that Afro-Christians, through Franklinton Christian College, also had the opportunity to train leaders for their communities and churches. The fact that black Congregationalists were able to sustain their educational programs longer than were Afro-Christians resulted far more from cultural and economic factors than from any intrinsic differences between the two groups. Black Congregationalists and Afro-Christians share the same heritage, come from the same places, and survived the same history of oppression and dehumanization.

We are not talking here either of de-Africanizing people to become Congregationalists or of reaffirming and claiming an African heritage to continue as Afro-Christians. The problem before us was, and remains to be, how to find effective ways of sharing religious discoveries and remembering our cultural heritage.

Both the black Congregationalists and the Afro-Christians have important contributions to make to the religious community. The former affirms clearly that to be a black person does not place limitations on one's intellectual or cultural abilities. With equal pride, the latter affirms that black people's identity and heritage continue to provide meaningful avenues of expression and self-esteem that are important to each individual, as well as to the entire community of faith as it bears witness to its past and its future.

How SCOPE Works

The SCOPE program seeks to draw on the strengths both of black Congregationalists and Afro-Christians to provide an alternate route to ordination within our conference — one that might even have application in the wider denomination.

There follows an outline of the program that was designed in 1988 by the Southern Conference of the United Church of Christ in cooperation with Lancaster Theological Seminary in Lancaster, Pennsylvania.

A. NAME OF PROGRAM: Southern Conference Ordination Preparation Education (SCOPE), An Alternate Route to Ordination, Full Ministerial Standing, and Vocational Enhancement in the United Church of Christ.

B. PURPOSES AND EDUCATIONAL PHILOSOPHY OF THE PROGRAM: SCOPE is conceived as a formal educational supplement to the extensive experiential preparation for ministry that some persons obtain in the UCC. All participants in SCOPE must:

   1. have publicly declared their calling;

   2. have associated themselves with a congregation as assistants, or in other pastoral roles;

   3. have, in fact, served as assistants (or in other pastoral roles);

   4. have been acknowledged by the Commission on Ministry as persons "in care" for preparation for the ordained ministry of the UCC;

   5. have been generally deemed by the congregations where they serve to be in process of becoming acceptable candidates for recommendation to other churches as pastors; and

   6. seek an educational supplement to their experience through the SCOPE program.

The SCOPE program is designed to allow the applicant:

   1. to obtain knowledge and skills that are essential to the practice of parish ministry in the UCC, but that are not readily obtained by experiential training alone;

   2. to achieve ordination when normal preparation through college and seminary education is deemed impossible;

   3. to prepare for ordination while continuing to be involved in the practice of pastoral ministry;

   4. to learn the value of lifelong education;

   5. to experience education as a resource for the practice of ministry and not as an obstacle to advancement in the church;

6. to appreciate how the educational experience might serve to improve the candidate's ability to minister effectively;

7. to be able to articulate the strengths of experiential training as legitimate preparation for ordination in the UCC, and to appreciate the training of persons who have chosen other routes to ordination.

8. to integrate four aspects of their preparation for ministry:

   a. Experience in the work of the church;

   b. Experience and training in secular areas of employment;

   c. Academic training;

   d. Personal faith experience within the church.

9. to participate as ordained ministers who are seeking to improve their effectiveness.

SCOPE allows the Association Church and Ministry Commissions:

1. to supervise persons "in care" and to observe their degrees of ministry;

2. to provide future ministerial candidates with counsel and guidance in their educational journeys;

3. to influence the curriculum studied by participants;

4. to coordinate the Conference commitment to provide education for persons who are seeking ordination, but who are unable to attend college and seminary;

5. to appreciate and accept fully the capabilities of those persons who have trained for the ministry primarily in experiential ways.

C. ENTRANCE REQUIREMENTS

In order to be eligible to enter the SCOPE program, an applicant must:

1. have earned at least a high school diploma or its formal equivalent;

2. be a member of a UCC church and be serving a pastoral role in it;

3. be seeking full ordination and anticipating a pastoral career in a parish setting;

4. have obtained approval of the Church and Ministry Commission for participating in this program;

5. be at least thirty years of age;

6. be able to demonstrate why college and/or seminary is not presently feasible;

7. have the recommendation and covenantal support for entry into SCOPE from the congregation in which the candidate serves.

In cooperation with a staff person and advisor appointed and approved by the Association's Church and Ministry Commission, each participant designs and presents a written plan for the year's study. The plan must include all topics listed for the unit of study being undertaken. The written plan serves as a contract between the participant, the administrator of the SCOPE program, and the Association Church and Ministry Commission; it must be approved by each party.

Assumptions Underlying the SCOPE Program

The designers of SCOPE identified the following assumptions that underlie the program:

1. The purpose of an alternate route to ordination, and of this entire effort, is to validate the gifts and skills possessed by certain candidates who cannot reasonably be expected to fulfill the preferred seven-year route that involves completion of both college and seminary.

2. SCOPE is not a degree program, nor should it be regarded as a substitute for the traditional, preferred route to ordination, the value of which is strongly affirmed.

3. SCOPE candidates, for the most part, are persons who have already established a relationship with their Association Church and Ministry Committees, and, in many cases, are currently serving congregations.

4. There will be a diminishing need for this program as the church develops the means by which to provide adequate support for all qualified candidates in the preferred college-plus-seminary route.

5. A variety of educational opportunities will be recognized or conducted by this program, and these opportunities will take place in a variety of forms and settings. Local resources will be emphasized.

6. Although stated in academic language, the standards and expectations of the program will not necessarily be fulfilled in an academic mode.

7. SCOPE's intent is to prepare candidates to serve as effective ministers and leaders in the congregations to which they are called. Forms of learning will be designed that are consonant with this intent.

8. Each candidate will be assisted in designing her/his own advancement toward the fulfillment of the program's requirements. A mentoring relationship between SCOPE and DMin candidates is necessary.

9. SCOPE will seek to motivate alternate-route candidates to continue their educational efforts after fulfillment of the program requirements.

10. Levels of understanding and competency will be evaluated.

11. The cost of the total program will be borne by all the participating parties: Conference, Associations, seminary, the Board for Homeland Ministries, degree candidates, and alternate-route candidates.

12. Educational opportunities provided through this program would be available to participants other than candidates for ordination.

Preparation for Ministry

We in the black church have a great and glorious tradition of competent, even prominent church leaders who, having been called of God, needed no more than to leave off gathering sycamore fruit, or to have their lips touched by the divine coal, in order that they might go forth and prophesy in God's name.

Indeed, the black church had its genesis, not in the ivied halls or cloistered forums of the universities, but rather in the faith of unlettered black men and women who heard themselves called, called to stand before their neighbors, gathered in swamps and bayous, and there to preach God's promised liberation. And preach they did, though they had never seen a book and no one had ever taught them the art of homiletics.

Their theology was a living experience intuited during prayerful walks with God among endless cotton rows. And their theology generated a faith on which the people built and created for themselves a great tradition and a great church. It is that same black church of which we are so justly proud and in which our confidence is lodged for today and for tomorrow.

New ways and new methods and new schools and new workshops and new plans must be explored in order that we may continue preparing candidates for ministry in the black church today. But whatever we do, we must stay as close as possible to the history that has inspired and sustained and nurtured this church over its long history. Our pilgrimage in America was made less onerous because of the unlettered men and women who have been our preachers and leaders in the black church.

Notes

1. Lawrence W. Levine, *Black Culture and Black Consciousness, Afro-American Folk Thought from Slavery to Freedom* (Oxford, London, New York: Oxford University Press, 1977), 89.

2. Charles H. Long, "Perspectives for a Study of Afro-American Religion in the United States," *History of Religions* 11 (August 1971): 65.

3. Eugene Genovese, *Roll, Jordan, Roll* (New York: Random House, 1976), 608.

4. Frederick Douglass, *The Life and Times of Frederick Douglass* (New York: Pathway, 1941), 111.

5. The National Conference of the Black Theology Project, "The Message of Black Theology" (unpublished, undated).

Four

Theology Among the People

*Theological Education by Extension
and the TAP Program*

RICHARD SALES

*Theology Among the People (TAP) refers to a program of theo-
logical instruction sponsored by the Southeast Conference of the
United Church of Christ. Course work combines instruction in
ministry skills with biblical and theological studies. TAP's original
intent was to make theological education for "licensed ministers"
in the UCC available to men and women who have not received
formal seminary education and who presently serve churches that
are unable to support a full-time pastor. TAP has several antecedents, including Theological Education by Extension (TEE)
and the Preacher Enrichment Preparation Program (PEPP). In this
chapter, I offer some insights into the historical context out of
which TAP arose and recount some details of the program itself.*

African Antecedents

In the early 1970s, Christian churches in the south African country of
Botswana faced a severe ministry crisis. The average age of a pastor was
over sixty-five. The various denominational mission societies had built
seminaries in Africa, but only in the more developed nations of southern Africa, such as South Africa and Rhodesia (now Zimbabwe). But by
the early 1970s both South Africa and Zimbabwe had closed their borders to ministry students from Botswana and other independent African
countries. An aging clergy population and the complete absence of seminaries wherein a new generation of clergy might receive education —
these were the difficult facts that the Christian Council of Botswana 3
had to deal with in 1973. Because I was one of only two persons in

Botswana who had been on a seminary faculty, I was asked to help the Council solve the growing ministry crisis.

My concerns in undertaking this work were somewhat different from those of the Council, however. During the previous fifteen years of my ministry in southern Africa, I had been deeply impressed by people called "evangelists" — pastors who had little or no theological background. Evangelists were placed in charge of congregations and given the same duties as ordained clergy, but were given no vote in meetings and no opportunity to seek ordination. Not only did these pastors perform the same duties as their ordained brothers (all were then male), but they also worked for half pay or less. To my observation, some of the evangelists had better pastoring skills than many of the ordained clergy. When the Christian Council called on me to design a locally based theological education method, I immediately asked for and received permission to consider these evangelists as possible candidates for the new program,

As soon as I had taken the assignment from the Christian Council, I realized that we were facing a tough question: How could a program of theological education come into being apart from the *resources* of a seminary? To be frank, Botswana was a country in which congregations seldom had the resources even to pay pastors their full stipends, much less to fund a new interdenominational seminary. Perhaps the answer lay in already existing programs that offered theology by extension.

Previously I had heard of TEE (Theological Education by Extension) and read of the work Ross Kinsler was doing in Central America. I had met Ken Mulholland, who was also involved in these Latin American experiments, but I had no idea what these men did or how they went about it. When I learned that Ross Kinsler would soon visit Africa, I arranged for him to make a stopover in Botswana. The interview with Ross was challenging. He flatly refused to share the TEE materials with me, saying that any such materials must be tailored to the context in which they were used. He encouraged me to produce my own materials. Nevertheless, Ross did agree to instruct me in some aspects of the TEE program. For example, he described the small groups that met on a weekly basis, and he gave me some insight into various ways to craft materials that would lead students through the subject matter of biblical study and theology.

Later that same year I returned to the United States because my wife had taken ill. But before leaving Botswana, I obtained permission from the Christian Council Committee to set up a program modeled on that of the English/African seminary, which offered a Certificate in Theology for home study. The committee expressed eagerness for me to begin as soon as possible.

In mid-1974, after my wife's death, I returned to Botswana. Now I threw myself into designing and preparing the first courses of the fledgling program. Luckily I had help with this. (Originally I had accepted the Christian Council's commission with the provisos that I not be named director of the program, and that I would be provided with at least two colleagues from among the denominations that made up the Council.) And so it happened: in January 1975 a program modeled on Theological Education by Extension was launched in Botswana. At first the new program was named the Botswana Theological Training Programme (BTTP), but today it is known as Kgologano College.

My colleagues, the students, and I literally learned by doing. In the beginning there were four groups that met weekly. We had the ambitious notion that we would be able to provide everything needed for a Certificate in Theology as granted by the Federal Theological Seminary in South Africa.

Our progress reminded me of wandering through a densely planted garden, most of which we could not see at first, but whose beauties unfolded before us as we persevered. We discovered that our students were, in reality, *participants with us* in a bold enterprise. We worked hard to prepare the best materials we could. Over and over again we were astonished by how highly motivated adults were able to connect their life experience as church leaders with the material presented in biblical and historical theology. As much as possible we combined instruction in ministry skills with the study of biblical and theological sources.

For all our enthusiasm and confidence, however, we were quite apprehensive when we learned that Dr. Alan Miller of Bethany Seminary in Indiana proposed to visit Botswana. Under the auspices of a Theological Education Fund study, Dr. Miller was conducting evaluations of East African seminaries. He was willing to subject the Botswana Theological Training Programme (BTTP) to the same scrutiny he gave to established, traditional seminaries. To our relief and gratification, the results of his evaluation were very encouraging.

Dr. Miller cited many areas in which BTTP excelled. Among them was our emphasis on cooperation, rather than competition, among group members. Such an emphasis enabled us to *do ministry* while we studied. He liked our (necessary) focus on simple, vernacular English for people for whom English was not their primary language. By putting theology into the language of everyday use, he suggested, we were making the subject matter both more digestible and more useful to the participants. He did advise us to reduce the number of courses in the core program.

Dr. Miller also enumerated a few areas of weakness, which we immediately attempted to eliminate or revise as appropriate. For example, the lack of a theological library put students at the mercy of their leaders' competency. Even though participants were encouraged to be critical of what they read in our materials, they did not have available to them a breadth of reading material. Isolation posed a problem as well. Dr. Miller pointed out that, whereas the group process built into BTTP seemed to compensate for the spiritual formation that often takes place in a seminary setting, our small groups were isolated from each other. The groups, he suggested, would benefit from occasional plenary meetings. Overall, Dr. Miller said that seminaries would do well to embrace, rather than be critical of, programs such as BTTP.

In 1981 I left Botswana. I was profoundly impressed with what the extension method of theological education had accomplished in the lives of many people. Perhaps my happiest moment was when Evangelist Albert Toteng, able and willing to struggle with the material presented, became the first person to be ordained after completion of the BTTP.

My next assignment was in Zambia, where I helped develop a program called TEEZ (Theological Education by Extension in Zambia). Taking into account the Zambian context, I rewrote many of the Botswana materials and developed additional courses that were responsive to Zambian needs. In addition, I prepared individuals to lead groups in four different languages. Literally hours before the end of my term in Zambia, I completed the mimeograph stencils for the TEEZ materials. Both African programs, BTTP and TEEZ, continue to be active and both have grown in enrollment.

Bringing the Insights Home

When I returned to the United States in 1985, after twenty-eight years in Africa, I was convinced that the Theological Education by Extension method had a future in this country. Upon invitation by the Christian Council of Metropolitan Atlanta, I developed a TEE program in that city for pastors who were refugees from Haiti and other countries. My experience in Atlanta did not turn out to be what I had dreamed it might be. I discovered that TEE was regarded as a "third-world thing" that was simply not applicable to United States–born men and women. Nevertheless, before long, I came to believe that throughout the southeastern

United States there was an urgent need for extension-type theological education programs.

After moving to a pastorate in Birmingham, Alabama, I learned from a colleague, the Rev. Carl Flock, that in the Christian Church (Disciples of Christ) in Alabama, none of the African American pastors was ordained. Most African American pastors, I learned, served rural, economically disadvantaged churches. Because of financial considerations and family responsibilities, these pastors were unable to attend seminary. Carl Flock suggested that we establish a TEE program in our home territory.

Together with a committee that he brought into being, Carl and I designed yet another incarnation of TEE, this time with American pastors as the target student population. This program was, and is, known by the acronym PEPP (Preacher Enrichment Preparation Program). Although grounded in the pioneering work done in Africa and elsewhere, PEPP employs materials that were totally rewritten to fit the needs and the context of our southeastern United States. Presently the Alabama region of the Disciples of Christ has ordained twenty-one persons — male and female, black and white — who have completed the three-and-one-half-year program.

Theology Among the People

It seemed apparent to me that my own denomination, the United Church of Christ, was in desperate need of finding alternative ways of doing theological education. At that time, congregations in the Southeast Conference of the UCC averaged sixty or fewer members. Most rural and small-town churches could not afford to pay seminary-educated ministers. More often than not, these churches were being served by pastors who had little or no formal preparation — and who often lacked even basic familiarity with the denomination. The situation was further complicated by the fact that the UCC had taken progressive stands on social issues, such as ordination of gay and lesbian people, reparations to oppressed people, and capital punishment. In the southeastern United States, where church members' political views tend to be conservative, the UCC's stands were not popular. Some independent preachers serving UCC churches were known to have encouraged their congregations to break away from the denomination. An alarming number of UCC congregations were, in fact, going independent — or just going under.

In 1997, Dr. Timothy Downs arrived in Atlanta, Georgia, to serve as new conference minister of the Southeast Conference. Upon learning of the problems facing UCC congregations in the region, he urged the conference leadership to look beyond church renewal efforts and beyond starting new churches. He asked, "Why couldn't the conference sponsor a judicatory-based, alternative route to theological education for church leaders of all stripes and hues?" I told him we could indeed do it, and forthwith I retired from my pastorate so that I might help create such a program.

The following year, 1998, TAP (Theology Among the People) came into being — the fourth revised and updated version of Theological Education by Extension with which I have been associated.

The UCC Southeast Conference and Authorized Ministries

I would like to step back for a moment and comment on authorized ministries in the United Church of Christ (UCC). As is true in many other mainline Protestant denominations, the road to ordination normally proceeds something like this: A person discerns a call from God to enter the ministry. That call is subjected to testing, first at the congregational level. If congregational leaders agree that the person's call seems genuine, the candidate is recommended to the association (the term used for a judicatory in the UCC). If the candidate's call continues to be confirmed, that person must undergo a process of instruction and practice. In recent years the instruction stage has generally been identified with traditional seminary education: three years of graduate work following upon the successful completion of four years of undergraduate work. Within the seminary setting, a candidate's call undergoes further evaluation. If the person's call *still* receives confirmation, she or he receives extensive academic instruction and training in the practice of ministry.

Upon completion of seminary, the candidate returns to the association. At that level, educational qualifications are assessed, and further examination of the person's fitness for ministry takes place. Finally, if a congregation calls the candidate — and the association is convinced that this person is truly called and fit — ordination follows. He or she then becomes a cleric in the United Church of Christ.

The process described above represents the norm today in most mainline denominations. This process that leads to ordination is based on a set of assumptions, including the assumption that an ordained person will serve a congregation (or congregations) that is (or are) prepared to support the cleric as a full-time professional. On the other hand, some clerics, who are able to sustain themselves with other employment, serve small congregations on a part-time basis. Many small churches benefit from such an arrangement. Occasionally three small churches combine their resources to support a full-time cleric. But the UCC cannot simply place a minister in this type of yoked structure without the formal agreement of the congregations. Understandably, seminary-educated men and women (often burdened by student loans) tend to seek the higher-paid positions offered by large churches, which are usually located in urban or suburban environments.

The circumstances I have outlined have had a profound effect on Protestant denominations in the United States, and the Southeast Conference of the UCC is no exception. Our rural congregations have rapidly diminished in number. In the five states composing the conference, seminary-educated pastors serve only twenty-three churches. Several of these pastors depend on a spouse's income for half or more of their family budget. It takes a special kind of person to choose the insecurity of such an existence.

The TAP Approach

In the summer of 1999, when TAP began to form study groups, I discovered a curious phenomenon. We had planned the program as a way to upgrade the education of local pastors in rural churches. But, as it turned out, the majority of persons in each small group were not local pastors, but rather church members — men and women who wondered if perhaps they were called to a ministry beyond the ministry they exercised as laity. Evidently influenced by the selfless leadership of their own pastors, these men and women chose to enter TAP for further discernment of their call. Of the thirty-six TAP participants who enrolled in 2000, only ten belonged to the original target group of local pastors.

The laypeople who entered TAP had not received any congregational confirmation of their call to ministry. Nor did they enter the program with the explicit intention of pursuing one of the three authorized ministries mentioned above. The TAP Advisory Committee decided that the program would be open to any Christian seeking a solid theological grounding, but, in the case of a lay participant, the person's home congregation and appropriate judicatories should be made aware that he or she had enrolled in TAP. Further, the advisory committee urged the home congregation to give its assent to a lay participant in some covenantal way.

What I observed happening in TAP, I had seen three times before — in Africa and in the United States. The brand-new groups attracted people who leaped at the opportunity for theological education of a sustained and deep kind.

You can imagine the varied reactions of an association ministry committee upon learning that persons who did not aspire to candidacy were undertaking the same course of study (and doing as well) as were those seeking formal authorization. I believe profoundly that many of these laypeople will have a powerful and positive influence on the future life of their congregations and of their associations, whether or not they ever seek authorized ministry.

I recall one young woman who expressed delight at being enrolled in TAP, but who stated categorically that she would not preach; she was there simply to learn the subject matter. However, the introductory course in the program includes a stipulation that *every* participant preach at least once during the course. The members of the women's group in her church gave her much encouragement. After preaching her first sermon, she sat in wonderment as she received praise from her fellow students. "Maybe," she said, "I need to think about this more. I still don't want to be a preacher, mind you." Today that young woman actively pursues opportunities to preach.

In my experience with group study, adult participants experience excitement and enthusiasm as they share ideas and tap into the wellsprings of life experience. Such study also brings ministry issues into sharp focus. Once past the introductory stage, group members begin to trust and help one another; they share their doubts and apprehensions; they offer each other support and encouragement. I have long stood in awe of the way that adults respond to this type of sharing. Seldom have I left a group meeting without having learned something new about the context of theology in people's experiences. In the groups I have worked with in the United States, the participants rarely possess a common background — even if they come from the same congregation or similar ones. Each participant's encounter with the diverse life experience of fellow students can enrich the learning process immeasurably. Having become valued friends to one another, participants discover depths of meaning in biblical and theological study — meaning that goes far beyond the materials they have read in preparation for the meetings. The young woman mentioned above was encouraged and supported in her preaching efforts by the other group members, who were well aware that she was nervous and unaccustomed to public speaking.

If the effectiveness of the TEE method has a secret, it lies in the energy of its participants. In TAP, the participants are over thirty years of age (our rubric calls for an age of at least thirty-five); they are excited to be doing real theological study; they are willing to study on their own time; and they become prime movers in the educational process.

How TAP Works

The TAP materials, as well as those used in the other programs of which I have been a part, are carefully crafted. We do not seek to present the results of cutting-edge biblical research, but rather to provide participants with a reasonably comprehensive understanding of the subject area. Assigned reading for a given week seldom exceeds twenty pages. The method has been compared to preparing a meal for the participants. Giving people too much to digest can result in leftovers on the plate.

In the study workbook for each topic, questions are posed at intervals — questions that summarize what has gone before and stimulate thought about the relevance of the material. Answers are readily available, usually on the back of the following page. We recommend that participants build personal libraries, and the materials often include bibliographies for those who want to engage in further research. I encourage each group to critique freely what is read in the study notes; many participants, after some hesitation, do so regularly.

Each study workbook includes a skill component. For example, all participants begin with the Gospel of Mark and the textbook *Barclay's Daily Study Guide*. After we are underway, I request that each person prepare a sermon on the section of Mark assigned for that week. In that first course, no special guidance on preaching is provided, but, as the course proceeds, the group is asked to respond to each sermon, to answer questions such as "What did you like about this sermon?" and "Since no sermon is perfect, what would make this sermon better?" Participants begin to grasp that sermons represent a special kind of discourse that is meant to be heard, not read, and that should touch hearers with the truth of the gospel. After eight weeks, almost without exception, participants find they are eager for more study and more practice preaching. They better understand why sermons do or don't work, and they trust one another with their concerns and doubts. Remarkably, guided by insights from fellow group members, they also improve their preaching skills.

The Mark/preaching course has a term of eight weeks. All subsequent courses comprise twelve weeks. Each course includes a skill component as well as an information component. After the first course, the skill components appear in a guide. Participants study these guides on their own, so that they may improve their competence in such areas as teaching, counseling, and administration. A preaching guide accompanies each biblical course subsequent to the introductory course on Mark.

As anyone familiar with group process will agree, successful group formation depends heavily on regular attendance. Each group is free to choose the time and place of meeting. They do, however, covenant to meet each and every week. Anyone who is absent from more than one-fourth of the meetings in any given course will fail to pass. In cases where a participant has genuine and pressing reasons for absence, I have scheduled makeup lessons with that individual. In general, however, the TAP student must take responsibility for attendance, as well as for completing the assigned work. To ensure fruitful discussion within the group, I have set an arbitrary minimum of four members in each group.

Each study/skill course ends with an evaluation, one part of which asks participants to reflect on the course and on how well the group functioned. The remaining portions of the evaluation focus on the students' grasp of the subject matter and accompanying skill. No student who has participated fully in a course has ever yet failed the final evaluation. I tell the groups that I am much more interested in how they have grown and matured in the faith than I am in the number of points they receive on an examination.

How Theological Education by Extension Enhances Learning

I would characterize the study materials I have developed as "modular." Each week's assignment includes a reasonable amount of reading, with accompanying workbook questions. The student, at one sitting, can complete a page or two of reading and answer questions relating to the reading. This organizational approach has proved to be extremely helpful to people with full schedules at work and at home. Further, when the group gathers, it is likely that everyone will have completed the brief assignment. One participant may have completed twelve years of education and another may have earned a Ph.D. degree, but each has dealt with the same bite-sized section of course material. As group members exchange information and relate the material to their own ministries and lives, they are able to begin appropriating what they have studied.

I have observed that it is extremely important for groups to meet regularly, preferably on a weekly basis, in order to avoid accumulating a large backlog of material that needs to be covered in the group meeting. If meetings are held two or three weeks apart, students may not recall the material they have studied.

In my own seminary experience, students were fed ten or more weeks of material and then were given examinations that covered a vast amount of subject matter. I call that indigestion. I believe strongly that, although TAP participants cover less material in a year's time than do seminary students, they retain far more of what they learn and retain it in a more usable way. In addition to taking part in group discussion about the meaning and implications of the reading, participants also put their learning to the test in practical, real-life applications, such as preaching, teaching, and counseling.

During my seminary years, as I tried to distill what was important from the mass of reading material and the numerous lectures, I had to leave a lot of leftovers on the plate. As an editor of materials for a number of TEE programs, my task has been to determine what subject matter I considered essential to the TEE program, and then to stick with that decision. Clearly the TEE experience is unlikely to produce growing-edge researchers. But if participants find the subject matter relevant and useful, they should develop at least a basic competency in the fields covered.

Some persons have been critical of TAP and other such programs on the grounds that these programs make preparation for ministry "easy." I would point out that participants choose to undertake this course of study *in addition to* their various vocational, family, and church leadership responsibilities. Furthermore, academically, TAP offers no fewer than four courses in both Old and New Testaments — this in addition to courses in church history, church history and polity, biblical theology, and worship. Participants learn to preach, teach, counsel, lead meetings, and administer churches. Each person produces a research paper for the final Master's Class. But more importantly, participants typically find their study so exciting and fulfilling that, at the end of the program, they are eager to continue their journeys in theological education.

After forty-five years in the ministry, having dealt with both seminarians and TEE participants, I find that I am both humbled and deeply impressed by the quality of the people who undertake extension-type theological study later in life. Each week I drive 450 miles to meet with

TAP groups, and although I hate driving, the travel is more than balanced by the joy I experience working with TAP participants.

Having said all that, let me admit that TAP is a work in progress. I would like to offer elective courses, and I hope that in the future the program may be able to do just that. For example, a person preparing for a music ministry will not find much in TAP that is related to that field. Also, if a participant has a bias against late-twentieth-century biblical scholarship, TAP may not be appealing. (On the other hand, I have observed several TAP students who were initially opposed to modern scholarship, but who become advocates of this approach by the end of the program.) TAP does not present a social agenda. However, participants are free to discuss their social views in the context of group discussion. In fact, I do not believe one can study the biblical prophets *without* alluding to a social agenda.

Most critically, because a program such as TAP cannot require extensive reading, students are not introduced to the same breadth of theological and biblical scholarship as are seminary students. Fortunately, in any given group, many differing viewpoints are represented. Mature adults who take part in this type of study often have well-developed understandings of the world based on a wide variety of experiences.

An annual convocation was instituted as a part of the TAP program in response to two challenges: (1) the subject matter covered by the courses is, of course, limited, and (2) small groups located over a wide geographic area are *de facto* isolated from each other. These annual convocations have been both useful and helpful. But the fact remains that a day of "seminary" is not a semester.

Some students have dropped out of TAP. In my judgment, a few of these persons were not motivated to enroll in TAP by a desire to acquire skills and knowledge, but rather by a desire for recognition by the church. I recall a young man who was sent to TAP by a congregation that wanted him to gain authorization for ministry, but the young man did not find the study engaging. One woman told her group that she joined TAP because she needed a support group after a recent divorce. In neither of these two cases did their respective groups reject the students; both students rejected the program. In yet another group, the majority of participants is well into retirement and sees the program as an opportunity to reflect on their lives. Sadly, one member of the group would like to work toward an authorized ministry but is not finding it easy to tackle serious issues in this particular group.

I have attempted to give a balanced picture of the TAP program in the Southeast Conference of the United Church of Christ. For the great majority of participants it represents, in their own words, an opportunity to grapple with issues, to clarify a sense of calling, and to become equipped for practical leadership in the local church. After twenty-five years of involvement with this approach to theological study, I know one thing for certain: I need never fear the failure of the theological education by extension method — a method that makes serious study of the Bible and theology available to people where they live and work.

Five

Standing in the Wings
United Methodist Local Pastors
and Their Preparation

BERT AFFLECK

This chapter describes how and why the United Methodist Course of Study Schools came about. Special attention is given to the historical development, within Methodism, of the office of local preacher/local pastor and of nontraditional theological education. These comments serve as a backdrop for my personal reflections on the Perkins Course of Study School. I hope to clarify the process of theological education available to United Methodist local pastors — men and women whose circumstances deter or disallow formal seminary training.

When Claire Biedenharn felt God's call to the United Methodist ministry, she found herself struggling with apparently irreconcilable issues. She knew she could not afford seminary. Nor could she compromise her commitment to care for her family. Even if somehow she were able to pay for a seminary education, it did not seem possible to her that she could leave her husband and children for three years. But then there was the matter of God's having called her to ministry.

"My district superintendent," she writes, "had the answer, and it was Course of Study School. The United Methodist Church offered an alternate path to ordination that could accommodate second-career people like me."[1]

In fact, after completing licensing school and one year of courses in the Mississippi Extension Course of Study School, Claire received her first appointment as a United Methodist local pastor, becoming a full-time local pastor. During summers she attended Perkins Course of Study School at Southern Methodist University, Dallas, Texas, to complete her basic Course of Study work. With joy Claire says, "Thanks to Course of Study School I am able to balance what I love most—my family and my church."[2]

A Personal Note

I taught my first course in the Perkins Course of Study School, Dallas Texas, in the summer of 1972. I was asked to accept the assignment because of the absence of a colleague who was undergoing heart surgery. Little did I know that this temporary position would lead to some of the most satisfying experiences I have had during a long career of teaching ministers-in-training.

When I walked into that first class in New Testament, I was surprised to discover that most of the students were ten or more years older than I. Throughout our time together, they inspired me with their hunger to learn, their sense of joyful urgency to preach Christ, and a deep wisdom that seemed to issue from years of lay church membership.

I have truly enjoyed teaching religion and philosophy to undergraduates, as well as teaching theology to graduate students in the Perkins School of Theology. But I give special thanks for what I have learned about theology and ministry during the past three decades as instructor and administrator with the Perkins Course of Study School for local pastors. In this chapter, I hope to communicate my gratitude for all I have gained. I also seek to give my own perspective on the crucial and valuable role played by the Course of Study Schools in the life of the United Methodist Church.

An Overview of Course of Study

In the year 2000 Claire Biedenharn was one of approximately twenty-five hundred United Methodist local pastors receiving nondegree theological training. At this writing the count has increased to three thousand. These pastors are engaged in Course of Study, a twenty-course common curriculum prescribed by the General Conference of the United Methodist Church.

Course of Study Schools (COSS) are located on the campuses of eight United Methodist theological seminaries: Candler, Claremont, Duke, Garrett-Evangelical, Methodist Theological School of Ohio, Perkins, Saint Paul, and Wesley.[3] Because secular job responsibilities often prevent part-time pastors from attending summer sessions at one of the main COSS campuses, ten extension Course of Study Schools have been established. Located in geographical areas more accessible for bi-vocational pastors, these extension schools operate under the auspices of the United Methodist seminaries. (The extension schools are Alabama, Appalachian, Mississippi, and Tennessee/Holston as extensions of Candler; Indiana, North and South, as extensions of Garrett-Evangelical; Arkansas and North Texas as extensions of Perkins; and West Virginia as an extension of the Methodist Theological School of Ohio.) Other such schools may be approved by the General Conference of the United Methodist Church.[4]

The Course of Study Schools located on seminary campuses normally operate during a four-week period in the summer. Most such schools hold two two-week sessions, and the majority of students attend two courses each session — a total of four courses per summer. Classes include foundational courses in Bible and theology, as well as functional courses in practical ministries. During the time between COSS summer sessions, students are assigned significant preclass preparation to accomplish on their own. Under this program, a student normally completes the basic Course of Study in five years (while serving simultaneously as a local pastor). Some students may, in fact, take longer than five years to complete the curriculum, but full-time local pastors are required to do so within eight years.

In contrast to the seminary-based Course of Study Schools, the extension programs usually offer classes on weekends, allocating either two or three weekends to meet the twenty contact hours required for one course. Part-time local pastors who are actively serving parishes are allowed up to twelve years for completion of the extension Course of Study.

The Local Pastor

The local pastor is the contemporary term in United Methodism for someone whom John Wesley and early Methodists called the local preacher. The local preacher was selected from among Methodist laity to preach and provide pastoral leadership in the absence of a full-time "traveling preacher."

Neither ordained nor lay, local preachers throughout Methodist history have found themselves living in a state of ambiguity. Local preachers exhibited an important dimension of Protestantism's principle of the "priesthood of all believers," a principle that affirms the sacred value of the *Laos* as the whole people of God. A local preacher in England

and America typically lived among the people of a congregation and was available to meet both acute and chronic pastoral needs — especially during times when the traveling preacher was, of necessity, serving elsewhere. Whereas itinerant preachers may have only seen members of a congregation when they were on their best behavior — such as during times of revival — local preachers often possessed deeper insight into the pains and crises and joys of their parishioners.[5]

Local preachers, sometimes called supply pastors or lay pastors and renamed local pastors in 1976, have long been the unnoticed, unacclaimed ministers of Methodist history, called upon to maintain continuing ministries day in and day out: preaching, exhorting, teaching, and providing pastoral care. Early local preachers may have cherished their role in which they were subject to the ordained elders — the traveling preachers who carried sacramental authority and who were recognized as the pastors-in-charge. Today, however, although local pastors most often serve as pastors-in-charge of congregations, many still struggle with feelings of injustice and "second-class citizenship" that result when "clericalism" quenches the spirit and callings of faithful laypersons.

Historical Beginnings:
The Rise of Methodism in England

Eighteenth-century England saw the rise of a movement called Methodism. In the spirit of disciplined grace, John and Charles Wesley organized the people called Methodists to meet regularly in bands (small groups of five to ten persons) and classes (consisting of twelve believers). People gathered in these bands and classes in order to pray, read Scripture, hold one another accountable, care for each other, and pursue a Christian life of holiness and reform for all. Again and again within these small groups, leaders emerged. Some became local preachers, of whom some became traveling preachers.

The traveling preacher played a major role in the rapid rise and spread of Methodism in eighteenth-century England. Not surprisingly, John and Charles Wesley established the model for this role. Acting as itinerant field preachers and superorganizers, the Wesleys stayed on the move, invariably displaying apostolic fervor. It fell to local preachers to render the critical ministry that served the daily and weekly needs of Methodist societies. These men provided leadership and spiritual nurture for the Wesleyan groups called bands and classes. As the movement developed, it was customary for local preachers to preach regularly in meetings near their homes, whereas traveling preachers journeyed on a circuit and preached in many different communities.

John and Charles Wesley carefully supervised both traveling and local preachers. They insisted on strict observance of Methodist rules and on pure proclamation of Wesleyan doctrine. With an iron hand John supervised these nonordained, mostly uneducated preachers, many of whom were miners and factory workers. He insisted that they read and study extensively — not only his *Standard Sermon Notes on the New Testament* but his other books as well. (And John was a prolific writer!) Charles Wesley, noted hymn writer of the Wesleyan revival, at times applied even stricter rules for preachers than did John. Charles retained a particularly close alignment with the Church of England's norms for ministry. For that reason, he expressed reluctance to accept the "irregularity" of non-seminary-educated, nonordained preachers. John's passion for mission and reform in England prompted him to retain some preachers whom Charles would have set aside.[6]

Francis Asbury

One enormously gifted local preacher was Francis Asbury, who became a major force in the rise of American Methodism. Born in 1745 near Birmingham, England, Francis Asbury dropped out of school to apprentice himself as a metalworker. But his passion was stoked not so much by his craft as by revivalistic religion. Methodist preaching services, in particular, touched him deeply, especially the message of Christ as savior; the heartfelt, extemporaneous prayers; and the melodious, fervent singing. He joined both a band and a class. In both groups he found assurance of forgiveness and salvation.[7]

Before long, Francis was attracted by the possibility that, even without university credentials, he might become a Methodist preacher. He first tried his hand at reading Scripture and leading prayer in meetings. Then he progressed to "exhorting," that is, calling others to apply the preacher's message to their own lives. Eventually he began to be invited to preach. Acting as a local preacher both thrilled and awed Asbury. In a short time, although still working as an apprentice, he found himself preaching three to five times a week.[8]

At age twenty-one, Asbury received an appointment as a full-time traveling Methodist preacher. He never looked back. He studied hard so that he might preach clearly and persuasively. With only six years of schooling, he felt vulnerable in debate with university-educated clergy.

Again and again John Wesley's books helped him compensate for lack of educational credentials. Asbury matured into a preacher with passion and with a gift for winning souls for Christ. Evidently John Wesley discerned these qualities. In 1771 he authorized Francis Asbury to serve in the New World.

Methodism in the British Colonies

Before Asbury ever arrived in the British colonies of North America, clusters of Methodists had begun to gather. During the 1760s, Methodist men and women met in Maryland and New York under the leadership of local preachers. One such preacher was Robert Strawbridge, a strong-willed Irishman who, in the spring of 1766, formed Maryland's first American Methodist society, and who later planted Methodist beginnings in Virginia and Pennsylvania. These ministries were undertaken by Strawbridge on his own — without Wesley's knowledge until after the fact.[9]

In New York City, a Methodist class began meeting in the fall of 1766 under the leadership of Phillip Embury. Before emigrating to America, Embury, converted by John Wesley's preaching, had served as a class leader and local preacher. Embury started the class in New York at the urging of his cousin, Barbara Heck, who insisted that he do so lest they all "slide into hell." The class included not only Embury, Barbara Heck and her husband, John, but also "the Hecks' servant man John Lawrence, and their black servant woman Betty."[10] They were soon joined by Thomas Webb, a retired British army captain. Webb, complete with captain's uniform and green eye patch, cut quite a figure. His flair seems to have carried over to preaching. In response to Webb's sermons, membership in the class increased dramatically. Webb's popularity further enabled him to initiate Methodist groups on Long Island and in Philadelphia.

These early efforts on the part of Methodist laity, although enthusiastic, were highly disorganized. Some Methodists petitioned Wesley to send more experienced leaders to the colonies. In 1769 Wesley sent the first Methodist missionaries/traveling preachers to America: Joseph Pilmoor and Richard Boardman. Wesley authorized Francis Asbury, along with Richard Wright, to join them.

Asbury and Wright arrived in Philadelphia during the fall of 1771. Asbury enjoyed a long and fruitful ministry, first as a traveling preacher and later as the foremost bishop of early American Methodism. In the years before and during the American Revolution, his indefatigable evangelistic spirit drove him to traverse the eastern seaboard, visiting the rapidly growing Methodist community. He became the best-known Methodist in the colonies.

The Eucharistic Dilemma

During the years between 1769 and 1784, Methodist societies in America increased in membership from one hundred to almost fifteen thousand.[11] This growth happened despite the civil upheaval of the American Revolution and an ecclesiastical crisis, which centered on issues of sacramental ministry. The growing body of Methodist Christians faced an important theological question: How were Methodists in America to continue receiving the sacraments of Communion and baptism in the absence of ordained clergy?

Earlier, John Wesley had ruled that Methodists in the British colonies, as elsewhere, could only receive the sacraments from Anglican priests. But many such priests had returned to England when the Revolutionary War intensified. In many areas, therefore, Methodists went hungry for the sacraments because of a critical shortage of ordained priests. Wesley worried mightily about this Eucharistic dilemma.

Meanwhile, back in America, unauthorized sacramental ministries were, in fact, provided by a number of local preachers, notably Robert Strawbridge of Maryland and other preachers who served in the southern colonies. Francis Asbury sought to correct these irregularities. Strawbridge refused correction, but the southern preachers reluctantly suspended their sacramental practices while awaiting Wesley's solution to the problem. Schism was barely avoided.

Wesley took until 1784 to provide an answer. Based upon his study of practices in the primitive church, he concluded that the order of bishop does not constitute an order superior to that of presbyter/elder. Bishops, he reasoned, occupy a functional position that involves oversight, appointment of clergy, and administration of a geographical area (a diocese) or designated portion of the church. Wesley, therefore, saw himself first as a priest/presbyter in apostolic succession, and also as equal to an itinerant bishop, that is, an overseer, a general superintendent (his preferred term) of a certain part of Christ's body.[12]

Based on this reading of early church history, and without formal ecclesiastical authority, Wesley ordained two laymen, Thomas Vasey and Richard Whetcoat, presbyters. Wesley then authorized Thomas Coke, an ordained Anglican priest, to travel to America and serve Methodists there as "general superintendent." Wesley further authorized Coke to ordain Asbury.

In 1784, at the Christmas Conference in Baltimore, Coke ordained Asbury deacon, then elder. The nearly sixty Methodist itinerant preachers in attendance then elected Asbury general superintendent to serve jointly with Coke. Twelve other men were also ordained to provide sacramental ministries for Methodists. This conference marks the official founding of the Methodist Episcopal Church.[13]

Although named co-superintendent with Coke, Asbury was by far the stronger leader of the two. In 1787 he took the title of bishop — much to Wesley's dismay. Asbury apparently believed the title gave him needed apostolic and functional authority as he developed a pattern for ministry that could, and would, move west with the American frontier.[14] With martyr-like zeal, this former local preacher ruled American Methodists for forty-five years. After Asbury died in 1816, he was eulogized throughout Methodism, and some twenty thousand attended his interment in Baltimore.[15]

The nineteenth century saw more and more nonordained local preachers serving Methodist congregations. By 1812 they outnumbered the ordained itinerants by two thousand to seven hundred — a trend that would continue deep into the twentieth century. Most of the locals lacked formal education. They developed leadership capabilities through the exercise of lay ministry, learning by trial and error, and preaching when called. Some individuals, by their example, set higher standards of learning and leadership for local preachers. One such person was Ohio's first governor, Edwin Tiflin, a well-educated professional who felt called to preach but could not travel. Also, increasing numbers of traveling preachers located permanently for one reason or another (e.g., health, marriage); they surrendered their membership in the annual conference but kept their credentials as local preachers.[16]

All in all, the first century of American Methodism owes a great debt to the lay ministers who stoked the embers of faith to keep the fires of love alive in the people called Methodists.

Gaining Recognition

For the most part, local preachers in the Methodist Church have lived and ministered in a state of suspension — neither fully clergy, nor simply laity. As Methodism expanded in America, the issue of credentialing local preachers gained visibility.

General Conference in 1796 voted to grant deacon's orders to licensed local preachers who had completed four years of service. The 1812 General Conference ruled that local deacons could receive local elder's orders after serving four faithful years as deacons. Questions of salary, administrative authority, and vote in annual conference remained. Most local preachers functioned gladly without pay and at the behest of traveling preachers. They worked their farms during the week and preached midweek and on Sundays.

Although Francis Asbury expressed his respect for the ministry of local preachers, he favored celibate itinerants. He did not hide his displeasure when a circuit rider married and located to raise a family. He wrote that he preferred unfettered preachers who were married only to the Methodist ministry. He believed that Methodism's growth depended on the circuit riders. But the truth of Methodism could not be told without due recognition being given to the "persistent local preachers who sometimes outrode the circuit riders."[17] Their credentials were commitment and perseverance. Like understudies of featured play actors, local preachers stood in the wings, ready to preach in the absence of circuit riders, when the curtain call from God sounded.

The Development of Alternative Theological Education

During the eighteenth century, education to the Methodist ministry depended upon a mode of apprenticeship. Soon, however, Methodist leaders perceived a need for an improved educational system. In 1816, General Conference responded to this need by authorizing the Course of Study for preachers who lacked formal education. Candidates for ministry were to be examined not only on Wesley's *Standard Sermon Notes on the New Testament,* but also on selected books by other authors. (A study of these required texts reveals a great deal about the theological transitions that took place from 1816 until well into the twentieth century.)

In the twentieth century, even after the formation of theological seminaries, Course of Study remained the dominant mode for educating Methodist ministers.

In 1902 the General Conference of the Methodist Episcopal Church, South established two new means by which ministers could complete the Course of Study: Correspondence Courses and Preacher's Institutes.

Students could take courses either by mail through the Correspondence School or at midyear Preacher's Institutes.

The Correspondence School, organized by the denomination's Board of Education, was first located at Vanderbilt University in Nashville. Until 1914 the School drew upon Vanderbilt's theological faculty for its instructors. (Vanderbilt's church affiliation ended in controversy over control of the university in 1914.) The Correspondence School then moved to Candler School of Theology at Emory University in Atlanta.

By 1918 enrollment in Course of Study had increased to more than fifteen hundred students. Another Correspondence School was established at the newly formed Southern Methodist University (SMU) School of Theology (later to be named Perkins School of Theology).[18]

In the early decades of the twentieth century, Course of Study included two branches. The main branch served traveling preachers, those seeking ordination and full conference membership. The other branch pertained to local preachers. In 1886, a two-year course had been prescribed for local preachers. This course continued unchanged until 1918, when some revisions were made. In 1930 the standard training period for local preachers was raised from two to three years when a license-to-preach course was added to Course of Study.[19]

From its inception, SMU School of Theology envisioned its role to be one of offering theological study to both clergy and laity of the Methodist Episcopal Church, South. The Course of Study Office at SMU provided correspondence courses and held Preacher's Institutes (sometimes called Pastors' Assemblies or Western Training School). These educational opportunities principally served persons residing west of the Mississippi River who sought to qualify for ordination without a seminary degree. Candler School of Theology similarly served those residing east of the Mississippi.[20]

By 1926 only 12 percent of ministers in the Methodist Episcopal Church, South had completed a traditional seminary education.[21] SMU's Course of Study utilized theological faculty to evaluate correspondence courses and to teach in the Preacher's Institutes (or Assemblies). This close coordination between the School of Theology and the Correspondence School continued through the first three decades of SMU's existence.[22]

Perkins Course of Study School Established

In 1947, the Course of Study School (COSS) at Perkins School of Theology (formerly SMU School of Theology) was formally organized and established under the direction of A. W. Martin, professor of church administration and director of field education. Martin led COSS through its first nine years until 1956.[23] A former leader in Arkansas Methodism, he placed great emphasis upon the practical applications of the fourfold theological curriculum: Bible, church history, theology, and pastoral ministries. Through the 1960s, the Course of Study curriculum maintained this basic pattern, with the addition of course work in doctrine, historical theology, comparative religions, and ecumenism.

During the 1970s the Perkins COSS curriculum changed little; there remained required courses in Bible, church history, theology, and pastoral ministries. It should be noted, however, that Claus Rohlfs's leadership as director established the school at much higher standards than ever before.

A Personal Journey

COSS has been an integral part of my life ever since 1972 when I began teaching in the program. I taught two courses during most summers until 1983, when I became director of the program.

After the first year or two, I began practicing what has been called "adult learning," that is, to treat each learner as a person with potentially rich resources and knowledge, all of which need to be accessed and shared. I attempted to gauge the level of knowledge at which each student would enter the discussion of given topics. I sought to draw out the students' contributions, questions, and reflections rather than to duplicate what they already knew and understood about the subject at hand. Discussion, debate, and sharing came alive in class sessions.

I am aware that this educational approach is not uncommon today, but I had been initially guided by a deductive educational method, one in which lecture presentation was the norm. What I discovered through COSS was that an inductive mode of teaching helped students discover for themselves the value of historical-critical guidelines in the study of Scripture. More often than not, analogical discernment helped students break through the barrier of the past so that they could identify God's work in biblical times with their own experience. They began to perceive that the biblical story was also the story of their lives.

One memory stands out for me. In 1973 I taught a course in parish organization and administration that included fifteen Native American pastors from Oklahoma. There is no doubt that I was the one who benefited most from the class. These Oklahoma pastors introduced me both to the richness of their tribal cultures and also to the pain of their past, their heritage from the Trail of Tears, which wrested their forebears from their homelands and forced them to move west to Oklahoma Territory. Through the years, these particular students have continued to inspire me. Again and again they remind me that God calls us to protest injustice and never to rest passively in the face of inequity and cruelty.

These years of teaching became a watershed period in my life. Each summer at COSS reenergized me and inspired me anew to thank God for my calling to ministry. The stories (some quite dramatic) of how these men and women answered God's call prompted me to ask myself whether I was truly listening for what God wanted me to be doing with my life.

After nearly a dozen years of service as minister to McMurry College, Abilene, Texas, I felt led to a campus ministry and teaching position on a state campus with a majority enrollment of Hispanics; I also served a black United Methodist congregation in a Hispanic city. My experience as teacher in Perkins COSS with its diverse ethnic enrollment (Native American, African American, Hispanic, Euro-Americans) influenced me to move more deeply into cross-cultural ministries, which movement in turn prepared me to be a more effective teacher and director of the Perkins COSS.

Along the way I have been enriched by my interaction with other members of the Course of Study School faculty, a faculty that has included colleagues from varied backgrounds and with amazing accomplishments. The COSS curriculum, which is offered in both English and Spanish, has brought together, from across the United States as well as from other countries (Puerto Rico, Cuba, Costa Rica, etc.), clergy, professors, administrators, pastoral counselors, denominational executives, educators, and missionaries. Their stories and wisdom have made faculty meetings and social gatherings a joy to attend. I have realized ever more deeply that our shared work in Course of Study represents a truly vital teaching ministry. What we have done each summer has affected local pastors of more than two hundred congregations from more than twenty annual conferences — a challenging task!

In 1983 I succeeded Claus Rohlfs as COSS director at Perkins School of Theology. In my experience the school was well organized; it had a strong faculty and an enrollment of faithful and hard-working students nurtured by a sound vision for theological preparation. I wanted, of course, to preserve the gains of my predecessor.

I sought to direct the school out of a profound dedication to two goals: achieving balance between matters of head and heart, and encouraging a reasonable search for the truths that might enhance effective ministry of the gospel. These two goals led me to call for high academic standards — not as ends in themselves, but as ways of sustaining the deepest commitment possible to "God as love" (1 John 4:8) in all aspects of the school: students, faculty, curriculum, administration, teaching methods, community life, worship, and church-relatedness.

The Course of Study faculty at Perkins remained largely intact during my time as director (1983–2002). Each two-week session normally included ten instructors for the Spanish-language courses (plus one instructor for academic resources) and sixteen instructors for English-language courses (with two sections in each of the first three years). Several instructors were members of the theology faculty at Perkins. Others served as pastors, professors, or in other church-related positions.

Advanced Course of Study

The COSS gives primary attention to a basic five-year curriculum, the satisfactory completion of which leads to certification for most students. The certificate of graduation from Course of Study School qualifies a local pastor in good standing to continue serving a congregation under appointment from an annual conference.

Some graduates, however, move into Advanced Course of Study School in order to pursue ordination as elders and thereby to attain full conference membership. Acceptance into Advanced Course of Study requires a bachelor's degree or equivalent, completion of thirty-two hours of graduate theological work (or the equivalent), three to six years supervised probation, and annual conference approval upon Board of Ministry recommendation (in accordance with the *2000 Book of Discipline,* United Methodist Church).

Local pastors who enroll for Advanced Course of Study at Perkins usually attend summer and interterm master of divinity courses, without academic credit, but with the expectation that they will meet all requirements for each course.

Course of Study for Hispanic Ministers

The Spanish Language Section in the Perkins Course of Study School serves critical needs in a region with a rapidly increasing Hispanic population. Roy Barton served effectively as coordinator of this section for many years (1974–95). In outlining the history of the Spanish Language Section, he writes that 1914 marks the first year in which Mexican pastors received training at Lydia Patterson Institute (LPI), a Methodist secondary school for Mexicans and Mexican Americans in El Paso, Texas. The Methodist General Conference recognized this educational work in 1934. In 1946 the Methodist Board of Missions provided funds to enable ministerial students to attend Texas Wesleyan College of El Paso. In 1951 the LPI theology department was moved to Perkins.[24]

One of Roy Barton's outstanding achievements was the formation and development of the Hispanic Instructors Program. This fellowship of Hispanic ministers, scholars, and church leaders drew not only from the Rio Grande Conference of the United Methodist Church, but also from across and outside the United States. Under Barton's guidance, the Hispanic Instructors Program became a vibrant forum for discussion of Hispanic concerns and issues. The program also stimulated a great deal of creative work, including many important writings within the Hispanic Christian mission. I am not aware that any other Protestant body has addressed Hispanic Christian initiatives as effectively as have the Hispanic Instructors. The National Hispanic Plan for the United Methodist Church grew out of the work of this group. Moreover, from the Hispanic Instructors Program have come many members of the Spanish-language faculty at Perkins COSS.

Barton maintains that "Hispanic work could not survive without Course of Study persons."[25] As with non-Hispanic students, COSS offers a theological education program for those whose circumstances prohibit pursuit of a seminary degree, and graduates of COSS are qualified for appointment in the United Methodist Church. In Course of Study School, students examine their callings, receive mentoring for ministry, and become part of a collegial group that has energy for advocacy and that strengthens connections among clergy. Many instructors in the Spanish Language Section of COSS were themselves reared in Hispanic contexts; they are uniquely able to interpret for students the rich and varied heritage that informs what it means to be Hispanic.

After Roy Barton's retirement, Minerva Carcaño succeeded him as director of the Mexican American Program. As coordinator of the Spanish Language Section of Course of Study School, Carcaño provided excellent leadership in leading the Spanish language faculty. Moreover, she collaborated creatively with administrators of Spanish Language Course of Studies at Claremont and Garrett-Evangelical seminaries, especially in regard to faculty development, curriculum review, and cooperative possibilities with Methodists in Cuba and Mexico. Her successor,

Jeannie Trevino Teddlie, serves as codirector of Perkins COSS with Gary MacDonald, director of continuing education at Perkins.

The Curriculum

The COSS curriculum is divided into *foundational courses* in Bible (Hebrew Bible and New Testament) and theology (historical and contemporary), and *functional courses* that cover various disciplines involved in the practice of ministry. A student normally enrolls in one foundational course and one functional course during each two-week session. Students at Perkins are required to complete twenty-two contact hours per course.

In 2000 the curriculum underwent revision. The new curriculum begins with a statement emphasizing the importance of contextualized learning. The revised curriculum gives increased attention to historical theology, spiritual formation, pastoral leadership, social ethics, Wesleyan foundations, and theological reflection on ministry. Biblical offerings remain essentially unchanged, other than substituting the term "Hebrew Bible" for "Old Testament."

See the end of this chapter (p. 98) for a comparison of the 1978–99 curriculum with the 2000 curriculum.

The Ethos of COSS

Can COSS be culturally defined? Is there an ethos that characterizes the student community of the Course of Study Schools? While I find it difficult to pin down, I do believe that an ethos — an identity, an underlying disposition, a common spirit — can be discerned among persons involved with COSS. Naturally, no single ethos can incorporate every student. Nevertheless, over the years, I have perceived, within the community of persons who have been part of Perkins COSS, a demeanor, a behavior, a certain witness to the truth of this program that I would identify as its ethos.

At its deepest level, this ethos is a matter of the heart, a way of expressing a calling from trust in, and commitment to, God as revealed in Jesus Christ. Some might put it in terms of conversion, that is, a radical change born of a penitent spirit because of postponed obedience to God. Most local pastors express the hope that participation in COSS will help them learn the jeweled facets of what it means to wear the calling of minister; they anticipate that COSS will help them put on the grace that covers us, transforms us, and leads us to love as we never dreamed possible. Charles Wesley's "Wrestling Jacob" hymn recounts the heartfelt spiritual experience that took place in Charles's life three days before his brother John felt his "heart strangely warmed." To recall that hymn, " 'tis love, 'tis love" that we are about; " 'tis love, 'tis love" that guides us as we seek to go where Christ leads us.

The language I would use to describe the COSS ethos echoes the spirit of what Russell Richey calls the "evangelical language" of early Methodism, language recorded in the journals of both preachers and laity. "In the journals," Richey writes, "the Christian life was an affectionate and expressive affair. Preachers spoke with freedom; words uttered in great liberty produced tears; hearts were melted; souls found mercy and were closely knit in love; a new community of 'brothers' and 'sisters' defined itself over against the world and the distinctions of sex, class, position and race that ruled therein."[26] Earlier identified with southern revival cultures, such language in recent years has reached into the hearts and souls of many COSS local pastors through the "Walk to Emmaus" movement. A vibrant lay movement that seeks deep transformation of grace in the Wesleyan mode, Walk to Emmaus has produced a significant number of people who have felt called to the local pastorate. (At least this has been true of students at Perkins.)

Certainly an ethos such as I have described does not preclude scholarship. In my experience, the majority of COSS students, even if they identify with a heart-centered religion, recognize the importance of study and learning. Most would agree with Charles Wesley's call to "unite knowledge and vital piety."

The ethos of COSS engenders significant bonding among local pastors. During each summer session, a community is created wherein members truly care for each other and learn how to enact self-giving service both within and outside of the COSS community. Mutual care and service are expressed in specific contexts: informal small groups, scheduled classes, worship, service projects, and student council meetings and activities. Often participants grow in an awareness of the need to nurture this type of bonding among people across the nation and around the globe.

Over the past thirty years, enrollment at Perkins COSS has been between 170 and 200 students. Most local pastors come to us from annual conferences throughout Texas and the surrounding states. But Perkins COSS has also drawn a good number of students from across the country and even from outside the United States. The students embody a cross-section of American society; they come to us from a wide diversity of professions and backgrounds. Most of our students are forward-looking and capable. Some are anxious and fearful about the requirements for completion of COSS; occasionally they are leery of encountering "liberal" ideas. Some have never attended college or university, others have not attended classes on a campus for many years. Although we provide counseling services, it very often happens that, with respect to daily stresses and strains, the students minister to one another.

Perkins COSS students are, on average, fifty years old. Not surprisingly, the majority of them, in addition to their work at Perkins, carry full responsibilities of job, career, and family. And, of course, as local pastors serving so-called part-time pastorates, many are consumed by heavy "people needs" in their home congregations. Seeing these fine men and women successfully complete COSS, aware as I am of the burdens they have borne for years, I know there is a God, a God of grace whose providential hand has made it possible for these students to overcome seemingly impossible obstacles in order to fulfill their goals and their calling.

Conclusion

Any valid history of Methodism should include the story of local preachers and pastors — how they have achieved theological preparation and how they have contributed to the church at large. I hope this chapter has illustrated possibilities in this regard. As both instructor and director of Perkins Course of Study School, I have experienced firsthand the truth that local pastors represent a long tradition of those "standing in the wings" ready to preach and to serve when their call from God finally connects. Theirs has been a precious gift to the church.

Some years ago there existed in our denomination the point of view that the Course of Study program should eventually be replaced by seminary education — or at least that the demand for Course of Study would diminish significantly as more and more ministers received traditional seminary education. And, in fact, beginning in the 1940s and continuing into the 1990s there was such a trend away from the Course of Study program. However, the end of the twentieth century saw two phenomena that resulted in an even greater need for local pastors: (1) the retirement of a significant number of active clergy and (2) a decrease in persons seeking to enter the ministry via the traditional seminary route. During the 1990s, Extension Course of Study Schools were established in order to educate the many pastors who were being called upon to fill vacant pulpits. At the same time, enrollment increased in several of the seminary-based COSS.

I believe a strength of the United Methodist system is that, in situations where there is urgent need, capable laypeople can be tapped for ministry. At this time a local pastor may be appointed pastor-in-charge of a church or of a group of churches. Unlike local preachers of the past, today's local pastors may receive salaries; sometimes they are provided with housing. They are permitted to vote as clergy in annual conference (except in matters pertaining to ordained clergy).

Present United Methodist polity allows a person to begin a preaching ministry under the following circumstances: recommendation by a local church; approval by a district committee on ministry and the Annual Conference Board of Ministry; and, finally, appointment by the bishop to serve under the supervision of a district superintendent. A candidate for ministry must explore his or her calling with an approved ordained elder, who also serves as a candidacy mentor. Furthermore, licensing school (eighty hours of training in pastoral ministry provided by a conference board of ministry) must be completed in order to qualify for admission to a Course of Study school.

There are situations where, arguably, local pastors have ministered far more effectively than seminary-educated and ordained ministers could have. Local pastors are often able to connect and identify with certain groups of people because they share that group's heritage or history. For example, Course of Study graduates have served essential roles in United Methodist work with Hispanic peoples, Native American communities, and foreign-language congregations, not only in the United States but also abroad.

Although local pastors have been called second-class citizens in the ministry, they deserve much recognition for undertaking frontline ministries in rapidly changing societal contexts. As my colleague Alex Joiner has pointed out, the passionate commitment of local pastors to making an immediate difference in their communities can empower ministry at all levels.[27]

My work with the Perkins Course of Study School represents one person's effort to help United Methodist local pastors gain theological education. Other accounts of COSS seminary-based schools would shed light on many different contexts and numerous creative endeavors. Stories similar to that of Claire Biedenharn abound. I recall the words of Sara Owen-Gemoets, another former student and also a recent COSS instructor: "We formed a very close-knit community. The fact that we were all second-career people who were very committed to ministry helped forge a bond that I have never experienced before or since."[28] I regret that limited space prohibits the recounting of these myriad stories, or, as Paul Harvey would say, of the "rest of the story."

Course of Study allows capable women and men to enter pastoral service, and, at the same time, to receive sound theological preparation. In many cases, these pastors have helped congregations not only to survive, but also to thrive.

CURRICULUM, 1978–1999	REVISED CURRICULUM, 2000
First Year	*First Year*
Pastor as Interpreter of the Bible	Pastor as Interpreter of the Bible
Pastor as Leader of Worship and Preaching	Pastoral Leadership and Administration
Pastor as Theologian	Theology in the Wesleyan Spirit
Pastor as Caring Person	Pastoral Care for Spiritual Formation
Second Year	*Second Year*
Preaching	Practice of Preaching
Exploring Our Heritage	Theological Heritage: Early and Medieval
People of God: Israel	Hebrew Bible I
Christian Education	Formation for Discipleship
Third Year	*Third Year*
Church Administration	New Testament I
People of God: the Church Evangelism	Theological Heritage: Reformation
Exploring Our Heritage:	Our Mission: Evangelism
The Wesleyan Movement	Pastoral Care and Counseling
Fourth Year	*Fourth Year*
Preaching and the Sacraments	Hebrew Bible II
Exploring Our Heritage:	Wesleyan Movement
Twentieth-Century Ethics	Worship and Sacraments
Word of God: Old Testament Books and Texts	Personal and Social Ethics
Fifth Year	*Fifth Year*
Church in Mission	New Testament II
Word of God: New Testament	Contemporary Theology
Performing Our Theological Task	Our Mission: Transforming Agent
Pastoral Counseling	Theology and the Practice of Ministry

Notes

1. Claire Biedenharn, "Written Account," unpublished, 2000.

2. Ibid.

3. The seminary-based Course of Study Schools are overseen by the Division of Ministry of the General Board of Higher Education and Ministry, United Methodist Church.

4. Funding for the extension schools derives from annual conference Ministerial Education Funds, whereas funding for the campus-based schools comes from general church Ministerial Education Funds.

5. Frederick A. Norwood, *The Story of American Methodism* (Nashville: Abingdon Press, 1995), 135.

6. Richard P. Heitzenrater, *Wesley and the People Called Methodists* (Nashville: Abingdon Press, 1995), 182.

7. L. C. Rudolf, *Francis Asbury* (Nashville: Abingdon Press, 1966), 66.

8. Ibid., 18.

9. Norwood, *The Story of American Methodism*, 66.

10. Dee E. Andrews, *The Methodists and Revolutionary America, 1760–1800* (Princeton, N.J.: Princeton University Press, 2002), 33.

11. Norwood, *The Story of American Methodism*, 74.

12. Rudolf, *Francis Asbury*, 47–48.

13. Norwood, *The Story of American Methodism*, 100.

14. Rudolf, *Francis Asbury*, 168–71.

15. Ibid., 219–20.

16. Norwood, *The Story of American Methodism*, 134.

17. Ibid., 135.

18. Lewis Howard Grimes, *A History of Perkins School of Theology* (Dallas: Southern Methodist University Press, 1993), 179.

19. Robert Sledge, "The Well-Furnished Minister: The Conference Course of Study in the M.E. Church, South, 1900–1939," in *Rethinking Methodist History*, ed. Russell E. Richey and Kenneth E. Roe (Nashville: Kingswood Books, Imprint, United Methodist Publishing House, 1985), 66.

20. Grimes, *A History of Perkins School of Theology*, 179.

21. Sledge, "The Well-Furnished Minister," 65.

22. As reflected in the archives of Southern Methodist University School of Theology.

23. Grimes, *A History of Perkins School of Theology*, 85.

24. Roy D. Barton, "History, Background and Function of the Course of Study in the Development of the Formation of the Hispanic Local Pastor," unpublished paper presented in the Consultation on Course of Study Schools in Spanish, 1998, in Nashville.

25. Ibid., 4.

26. Russell Richey, *Early American Methodism* (Bloomington: Indiana University Press, 1991), 84.

27. Alex Joyner, "Reflections on 5 years of Teaching in the Perkins Course of Study School," unpublished statement, 2000.

28. Sara Owen-Gemoets, "Memories of Course of Study," unpublished statement, 2000.

Six

Shall We Dance?

*Living the Adventure That Is
New York Theological Seminary*

MINKA SHURA SPRAGUE

In this chapter, I offer my interpretation of what we do and how we are at New York Theological Seminary. I hope my reflections will resonate with the experiences — or dreams — of others, particularly those engaged in locally based theological education. I am actually seeking to highlight the odd things that underlie or inform the way we are in God's world. And I am humbly aware that my voice is utterly particular, specific, individual. (Such an overview would take very different shape if seen through various of my colleagues' eyes — though one body, we are all so different from one another!) Nevertheless, I pray that my assessment and exploration of the NYTS tradition will honor those with whom I serve, as well as those who have gone before.

For these past hundred years New York Theological Seminary (NYTS) has been located on the island of Manhattan. In 2001 we celebrated our one hundredth anniversary as an interdenominational Christian institution. Founded by Wilbert Webster White as The Biblical Seminary in New York, NYTS now grants accredited master of professional studies, master of divinity, and doctor of ministry degrees; it also awards a certificate in Christian ministry.

This profile may sound mainstream enough, but, in fact, we were born with a very particular vision that has led us in some rather unusual and groundbreaking directions. Along the way, many of us have used the symbolic language of "pilgrimage," "wilderness," "stepping out in faith led by the Spirit." If a bridge between traditional theological education and locally based theological education exists, New York Theological Seminary stands squarely on that bridge.

For the first seventy-five years of its life, NYTS owned land. The seminary operated a traditional residential campus. Then, once upon a time in the 1970s, under the direction of George Williams Webber, we actualized Jesus' advice in Mark 10:21: "Go, sell what you have." The leadership of NYTS held tight to God's promise of resurrection as the seminary gave up all of it: the campus, the library, tenured faculty, even accreditation for certain degrees. For the next twenty-five years, we rented our primary space from the Marble Collegiate Church, sharing library and classroom facilities with the General Theological Seminary, which is located in a nearby neighborhood. And today, once again, we are holding fast to God's providence as we seek to leave Marble Collegiate Church and pitch our tents elsewhere. As of this writing we are still negotiating for suitable facilities.

A sense of emancipation was in W. W. White's heart when he founded NYTS. This new educational institution, he insisted, was to be "emancipated from shabby superficialism, sterile intellectualism, sectarianism, provincialism, and [geographical] sectionalism." White placed the Bible at the heart of the curriculum and adopted inductive educational methods for academic instruction. Inductive education emphasizes personal study and interpretation rather than lecture-style input. The inductive method is an interactive one in which the teacher's role is one of guiding students through an encounter with the material.

Today, like many other theological schools, we follow a fourfold theological curriculum of biblical, historical, theological, and pastoral studies for the master-level and certificate programs. We offer in-field education programs and give credit for Clinical Pastoral Education training in hospital chaplaincy.

On the other hand, to accommodate the working and weekday schedules of our students, most of our classes take place in the evening and on Saturday. Issues of ministry and church life lie at the heart of all course work at NYTS. Faculty members travel to Sing Sing, a maximum-security correctional facility in Ossining, New York, to teach courses that lead to one of our master's degrees. Our seminary students participate in programs for youth who are running easily and well in their neighborhoods and for youth who are most at risk. Inside what looks like a traditional MDiv curriculum, there are required courses in exegesis and social analysis, that is, methods for "reading the world." Many of our studies can be done in the Korean and Spanish languages as well as in English.

The Bible Is Our Meeting Place

I have been professor of New Testament and Biblical Languages at New York Theological Seminary since January 1987. Prior to this appointment, I completed a ThD at The General Theological Seminary in New York, taught at NYTS as an adjunct professor, served in a local congregation, and was ordained deacon (Episcopal). For the record, I have also packed school lunches, made Halloween costumes, and done the best I knew how mother-wise. My growing-up years were spent in the Great Plains, on the western side of the Mississippi River, out there in Liberty, Missouri, right next to Kansas.

When I joined the faculty of NYTS in 1987, I learned that a full faculty appointment here mandates weekly Bible study with one's colleagues. I thrilled to this requirement; I still do. I slid into weekly Bible study as easily and comfortably as I would into old and familiar clothes. Our founder W. W. White intended that the seminary seek to empower ministerial formation that transcends our various doctrines and divisions. White made use of contemporary inductive education in building the curriculum of The Biblical Seminary in 1900. Bible study from every perspective imaginable served as the basis of all study. Since then, weekly Bible study has served as the heartbeat of the entire NYTS community (whether one serves in a teaching, learning, or administrative role). We do not share living space; we all dance between congregational and academic institutions; we are a medley of denominations and ethnic origins. The Bible is our meeting place, our common ground.

In my first semester at NYTS I had my socks knocked off in, of all places, a monthly faculty meeting. As the new kid on the block, I was assigned to record the minutes. I was not prepared, however, to record something as surprising as a decision to offer the MDiv degree in Spanish and Korean as well as in English. I recall that phrases like "Why not?" and "How do we know unless we try?" landed on the table.

I had never seen such a thing in my life. For eleven years I had been at The General Theological Seminary, studying for two degrees and doing continuing-education administration in my spare time. I had taken classes uptown at Union Theological Seminary and also at Jewish Theological Seminary. I had tutored and instructed at both GTS and UTS. I was no stranger to the inner workings of seminaries.

Even though adjunct teaching at NYTS had already shown me the excitement that multicultural classrooms and colleagues can bring, I had never once imagined the educational adventure that NYTS had in store for me. So, when the faculty voted to offer the MDiv degree in Korean and Spanish, those famous words from The Wizard of Oz landed in my head: *Dorothy,* I thought, *you are not in Kansas anymore!*

Since the decision to offer the MDiv in Korean and Spanish, we have, of course, revised and redesigned *everything* — and, not surprisingly, done it (what seems like) a million times. We have admitted mistakes as well as celebrated successes. Our hearts have been broken and healed and broken again. From our lips has come our own version of grumbling — grumbling because there is no garlic on the way to the Promised Land. We have sat through Bible study after Bible study and continued to ask questions like "Why not?" and "How will we know unless we try?" and "If not now, then when?"

Today, I have a decade of teaching at Sing Sing Correctional Facility under my belt; I have my own feelings about what it is like to go "up the river" to teach. For this new millennium, NYTS has designed a program for urban youth that is implemented by a coalition of New York City congregations, MDiv students, and many alumni from our prison program.

On occasion, I have felt as if I have arrived at the Promised Land and, yes, it is everything that was promised. At other times, I have been very aware that, in the Promised Land, I haven't the slightest idea which berries are poisonous or which path to take; and then, there is that lamentable absence of garlic! Certainly it has never been dull; of course, neither was Kansas when I grew up out there on the other side of the Mississippi River. But it's pretty clear to me that I'm not in Kansas anymore. No longer in Kansas and on a bridge between locally based theological education and everyone else — however did this happen to me?

Oh, Freedom!

Our founder's intentions at the birth of NYTS provide an excellent beginning point for some reflections that dance in and around various biblical texts that now run through my veins. White's insights resonate with the very beginnings of Christian faith communities.

When W. W. White called The Biblical Seminary into existence, the War Between the States was within generational memory and women had yet to achieve suffrage. As I have previously indicated, White was adamant that this new educational entity be "emancipated from shabby superficialism, sterile intellectualism, sectarianism, provincialism, and [geographical] sectionalism." Evidently White found other forms of theological education too head-oriented, too regional, too denominational. He yearned for huge horizons; deep waters; thick, rich forests. His vision and his use of the then-innovative method of inductive education altered even the *shape* of the courses. He sought what today we call "holistic" learning — education that resonates within the student's body and spirit, as well as within her mind. He sought theological education that was *relevant* to the life of the church. At the seminary's centennial celebration I heard echoes of these widening horizons, deep waters, and richness of tradition in the stories told by Biblical Seminary alumni. In their stories, I could hear the freedom that was White's dream.

If we are to achieve emancipation, we must look diligently for everything that binds, that limits life. Before we can envision our lives, much less formulate "mission statements," we need to identify everything that limits our horizons. To be human is to bind *ourselves* to our lives.

Biblically, this tendency towards self-enslavement has clear precedent in the very first Christian generation. The Apostle Paul is outraged when he writes to one of the fledgling faith communities that has been established in the outer reaches of the Roman Empire. In the 50s of the first century, Paul writes to the Galatians: "By way of freedom, Christ has freed you. Stand therefore, and do not again become entangled by a yoke of slavery" (Gal. 5:1).

This is, of course, easier said than done. Like the Galatians, we are always susceptible to slavish entanglement in our work, family life, personal habits, and faith practices. "Watch it!" the Apostle admonishes. Near the end of the letter (Gal. 6:15), he is very clear that what is at stake is "a new creation." In the light of the crucifixion/resurrection experience, it becomes our human responsibility now to move by the power of the Holy Spirit and *choose emancipation.* It is no coincidence that the biblical word (*apolutrosis*) that we translate as "redemption" literally means *manumission,* technical release from slavery. *Apolutrosis,* or release from being counted as the property of another human being, is what Paul is talking about. Included in Paul's letter to the Corinthians, and later in the letter to the Romans, *apolutrosis* was just as important a concept in first-century society as it is today (1 Cor. 1:30; Rom. 3:24; 8:23). The cross of Christ purchases our freedom from *ourselves.*

Over and again, in every body and in every generation, we are called to set ourselves free from ourselves. If a generation can be counted as twenty years, then at New York Seminary, we are in our fifth generation — and each day we continue the search for our shackles. Interestingly enough, in this time of relocation, they are regularly visible. There is nothing like a physical move, an uprooting, to call up every dependency, every habit, every fear of change. And, in that moment, we see how truly bound we are. The only worse thing would be for us to *choose* slavery, thereby proclaiming Christ's sacrifice to have been (for us, at least) in vain.

Just Who Are We Anyway?

It is said that the body of Christ incarnates wherever two or three are gathered together. Jesus promised this faith reality — a reality that can only be appropriated by way of the power of the Holy Spirit (Matt. 18:20). Ostensibly, who we *are* — in any locale, at any time or place — matters! We both become *and* bear the Word by means of his very present incarnation — Word become flesh, full of grace and truth (John 1:14).

NYTS is altogether locally based. This incarnation of institution depends, for its constituency, upon the faithful community of the greater New York City area, a population that constantly changes. Presently our students number several hundred; about half are women. Most students are of African American and African-Caribbean American descent. Korean Americans and Hispanic Americans make up another large percentage; those of European descent are in the minority.

At NYTS we work continually and diligently to represent our wider constituency — in curriculum design and course offerings, in faculty and staff appointments. Actually, this is the easy part. It is much more difficult to ensure that all these voices are lifted and singing, making "earth and heaven ring with the harmonies of liberty." And, even so, it is far easier to *sing* James Weldon Johnson's fine words than it is to take time, to accord value, and to share power and authority.

The reality here is that, although we are many and diverse, nevertheless we are always functioning in the English language. And within English words (as is true of any language), there are a million assumptions and presuppositions, great subtleties, various elemental philosophies, and (of course) a shocking capacity for misunderstanding. Moreover, centuries of injustice can threaten generosity at any moment. It takes enormous amounts of time and patience for our community to communicate, to be *one* body.

Sometimes misunderstanding can be hilarious. My biblical field colleague is from Korea. We discovered, the hard way, that our respective peoples do not assign the same interpretation to the expression, "God knows." We had worked together for weeks before I learned that, for my colleague, this expression implies "everybody knows." I had assumed that he shared my idea that the words connote "nobody knows." Fortunately, we talk enough to get our divergent understandings out on the table. Today "God knows" is, for us, an idiom that invariably calls forth good-natured laughter from us both.

Here's the thing: taking and making time to be the body of Christ constitutes the whole ball game for me — whoever, wherever, however we are. Further, I think it behooves us unceasingly to ask who is *not* present, who is *not* represented. NYTS may not own real property but we are, nevertheless, locally based. Uprooted and moved out of the New York City area, we would not be ourselves. Because we are a port city with an ever-changing population, our diversity comes naturally. But we must always ask, I think, *Who is missing?* Jesus told us to do this — to go to everywhere and bring everyone to the feast (Luke 14:21).

According to NYTS oral tradition, an earlier passage from Luke "got us into jail," that is, started us teaching in the prison. As the story goes, discussion around the table was focused on Jesus' reading (in the Nazareth synagogue) of that peculiar passage from Isaiah. Reportedly someone at the table said, "I can see how to bring good news to the poor, sight to the blind. But how do we set the captives free?" Someone else is said to have answered, "Maybe *we'll* have to *go to them*" (Luke 4:18). That's what we did. We have never been the same since.

Inevitably, in our conversations, some voices are missing. At times there are voices that sound but are not truly heard. Underneath apparent consensus, often there are unspoken assumptions that lead us, as individuals, in altogether different directions. We live with the reality that, in any given locale, a part of the body will likely be missing.

One, One Body by Christ

In the first Christian generation, Paul named *us* as Christ's body, a body that transcends all the barriers that are erected by most societies. Economic, racial, gender, class, religious barriers — all disappear in the strong claim of Galatians 3:28. But actually *being* this body within a society — united in spite of, and beyond, these barriers — is a fine trick.

Paul *names us* and then goes on, in 1 Corinthians 12–14, to talk about how we are to *live* as the body. To begin with, we are to take our roles seriously — "if you are an ear, be an ear" — and turn to Christ as the head. In the next Christian generation, Paul's disciple, the writer of Ephesians, presses this image even more vigorously: "One body and one Spirit joined and knit together by every joint with which it is supplied, when each part is working properly, makes bodily growth and upbuilds itself in love" (Eph. 4:4–16). I believe we are being called to think also in terms of the body that lies *beneath* the skin, that is, tendons, muscles, and joints. Within the visible body lie systems and structures that function together invisibly to make possible human life. Endocrinal, gastrointestinal, cardiovascular systems somehow know how to live healthily, and in harmony, without our even giving them a thought.

Institutional bodies have deep inner structures as well. If we are to upbuild ourselves by love — in our families, churches, schools — even the systems and structures we *cannot see* must function well. The author of Ephesians has taught me to look deeply: around the faculty table, in the classroom, in congregational meetings. "What is really going on here?" I find myself asking, striving to remember that what I see is not all there is. I fish for origins, seeking the paths that led us to this place. I speculate about the long-term effects of our actions. My image for these effects, or consequences, is one of ripples moving continuously outward, long after the stone has fallen to the bottom of the sea. I urge the consideration of "exit lines," graceful ways to withdraw when good ideas don't work.

When my heart has been broken, or when I have become enraged, I have learned to stay, to persist, to hold fast. In John 13–17, the body of the disciples is at table with Jesus. When Judas leaves, the body is broken. I struggle to stay in the body, stay at the table. "I am this body by the power of the risen Christ," I remind myself. Often I use the words of an old song: "Stay, just a little bit longer."

I think of this persistence as "setting my face toward Jerusalem." And if I gnash my teeth or stomp the pavement or cry, that's okay. Many emotions, I have learned, have a life span of about seventy-two hours. I pray that I might offer and accept forgiveness of myself and others, and that I might claw through the next seventy-two hours as best I can. It is no coincidence, I think, that the period of seventy-two hours represents three days, the time between crucifixion and resurrection. Staying three days helps to clear my mind and heart; for me, it represents a way to find the Way.

Our bodies have depth, and they are utterly mysterious. Truly Christ is the head of each one of us, and all of us *as* one. God alone, as far as I can see, knows what is going on a lot of the time. I cherish Horace Boyer's words, and I use them when I have no idea what is really going on, or what I am to do. A paramount performer of gospel music, teacher, and writer, Boyer once was teaching harmony to European American musicians when suddenly he took away everyone's sheet music. "Now," he said, "sing as close to each other as you can get, and stay out of each other's way."

Trolls under Our Bridge

In fairy tales, bridges attract trolls — horrid little creatures who delight in bothering anyone who attempts to cross the bridge. On the bridge between traditional and locally based theological education, we who are part of NYTS most definitely experience our share of trolls.

Trolls are the mean little tendencies and temptations that make us stumble in our mission. Trolls cause imbalance, they seek to make the one (the body) who is crossing the bridge fall. Any part of the body, either within or without, can cause it to stumble. And yet, there is a reason that trolls form an integral part of fairy tales. Remember that trolls and temptations also have their vocations, their reason to be. They call attention to the fact that we are crossing over. We are going from one place to another, and trolls help us clarify and choose.

We all know that *smugness* is a temptation, a predictable troll. Walking a different path successfully can very easily invite self-satisfaction. "How will we know unless we try?" can turn on a dime into "Anything you can do, we can do better." But we can't always do better; nobody can. This is earth, not heaven. None of us has all the pieces of the puzzle, and certainly none of us can be all things to all people all the time.

NYTS includes a dozen full-time faculty, and a blessed host of adjunct faculty nearby. Also, we have a small support staff. I often find it helpful to run a quick reality check on the time and energy of the support staff. Even in a technological age, energies and time are limited. Great program ideas can fail or fall flat without adequate resources of energy or time or money.

And then, just as we manage to get *smugness* in check, feelings of *inadequacy* and *second-class citizenship* often raise their ugly little troll heads. The only antidote to these, I suspect, is faith: taking time to find faith, in and through our own belovedness and our own forgiveness, and in the certainty of our mission. *We would not be doing this, were this not our call,* I find myself thinking. Then, I work to discover why I do not feel adequate in this instance, why today I am inclined to be defensive. *Intentions* and *motives* matter, even though we know that bad pathways can be paved with them. Once I am reassured that our intentions and motives are good intentions and motives, I love to envision Hollywood-style revivals — faith-healings for our sense of inadequacy!

Another troll that is always lurking under the bridge is *shifting the blame*. This may be particularly true for bodies that attempt to work by consensus. Leaders must have the courage to take responsibility, to take blame — even when it hurts (and it does hurt). If leaders do not take responsibility, the energy of whatever has happened, be it mistake or misfortune, keeps right on moving, gathering momentum as it goes. Recently I found myself teaching this idea in the classroom, begging students to participate in a school-sponsored event that I knew would tax their money and their time beyond endurance. "My fault, our fault," I kept saying, much as I hated it, wishing petulantly that I had actually *made* the decision that landed me in this predicament. Since then, I have discovered that General Eisenhower left a note on his desk before the D-Day invasion in World War II, taking full responsibility for any fault or failure that might occur; I would have told this story had I known it at the time.

The speed mechanic may be the most insidious of the trolls. "Hurry, hurry," this one whispers, "you must *fix it now,* this is your only option!" It takes absolute serious-mindedness to remember that we can always *take* time; we can *make* time. Serious-mindedness blended with faith in God's creativity helps me recall that there are *always* more options. Indeed, given time, options just plain do arise. I have learned that not taking time often results in our spending more time later *undoing* what we have done (that which would have been better left undone — at least for a time).

Trolls under bridges are a bad surprise. But I find comfort in this thought: trolls, like us, reside on earth, not in heaven. Watching out for them, expecting them, snatches from them a good deal of their surprise.

Everything Is Everything

Years ago, when I was doing postdoctoral work, Dr. Sara Little, a supreme Christian educator in the Presbyterian tradition, etched upon my soul the truth that "everything is everything."

A week rarely goes by that I do not have to remind myself of this truth: Nothing is ever lost, there is nothing too small for attention and care in God's divine design (*oikonomia* in Greek). *Oikonomia* is translated as "plan" in Ephesians 1:10. In that letter, human beings get to make "plans," and God has "an *oikonomia* for the fullness of time, to unite all things in Christ, all things in heaven and all things on earth." At every moment of every day, we stand in this *oikonomia;* we are an integral part of an enormous, eternal design — a divine design. To echo the very beginning of Scripture: Everything is good, utterly good, whether or not we can see it or feel it.

Metaphors help me turn and return to the truth of God's divine design, be it in the classroom or in the committee room. I think about icons — small, detailed pictures that seek to capture deep, eternal realities. Working in the moment, I create the best icon I can, praying like crazy that it will have a deep, eternal truth in the greater divine design. At other times, I think of *oikonomia* as an enormous jigsaw puzzle. I do jigsaw puzzles by first removing all the pieces from the box and turning them right side up. I put the cover of the box next to me and then begin looking for the corners. With regard to *oikonomia,* I dare say that God has both the cover of the box and the corner pieces to that puzzle! As I attempt to enact ministry, I take the few pieces of God's *oikonomia* that I have, assemble them, and then, wherever possible, join them to other people's pieces. "Without," as a colleague once added, "jamming them into place until the edges fray and they no longer will fit where they really belong." Beautiful mosaics are made the same way, carefully, mindfully, piece by piece.

It is a fine dance: living inside a picture, the totality of which we can never see. I hear the echo of an old rock-and-roll song by Sting. I cherish the promise that, in God's *oikonomia,* with every step we make, every breath we take, God is watching us.

If we are to assign value and meaning to the *oikonomia* and to our own individual lives, prayer, reflection, and evaluation are absolutely necessary to our embodied rhythms. Prayer, reflection, and evaluation change the very energy with which we breathe and move. This is, Greekwise, *katallages,* or "reconciliation" (at least this is the way Paul uses the word in 2 Cor. 5:18). In the first-century Roman Empire, *katallages* decidedly did *not* mean "make nice" or "get over it." The word we translate as "reconciliation" is the term used for changing money from one currency to another at the provincial borders. An exchange of currency has happened, by way of Christ, in our relationship to God, says Paul. And with every breath we take we have been given the ministry of making possible this kind of exchange.

None of us is complete in, or *of,* ourselves. For all of us, this is earth, not heaven. Locally based, surrounded by stone, on some bridge between these two kinds of theological education, we are all somewhere, somehow, in God's *oikonomia*.

This collection of essays, I submit, attempts to offer a selection of icons that presently exist within a very large picture. My own hope is to hammer out some words about the odd things I have experienced at NYTS — as we dance upon the bridge. For all of us, whatever model of ministry we follow, Paul's words of assurance to the Philippians may become our words of assurance as well: "I am confident that the one who began a good work in you will bring it to completion at the day of Jesus Christ" (Phil. 1:6).

When I wonder what is missing at NYTS, what is not here that might be here, I see faces in a great cloud of witnesses, and I hear prayer. Approximately 150 students begin our programs each year. I now remember nearly fifteen years of these faces, I hear fifteen years of prayers. Behind the faces — some joyful, some filled with pain, some behind bars — stand more congregations and families than I could ever number.

Long, long ago when I grew up on the western side of the Mississippi River, out there by Kansas, we square-danced. The colors and the sounds and the movements of square dancing leap into my mind when I think of the students and congregations and families and ministries that have woven in and out of all my years at NYTS.

One meeting of our supervised ministry group serves as a type of Polaroid snapshot of the reality I have repeatedly experienced. It is a Saturday morning meeting for MDiv students doing field education (there are three such gatherings each semester). The seventy-five or so students are joined by a team of ministers, who will lead small-group discussions. Today's group presentation and discussion centers around the NYTS program called *Uth Turn*.

Here is the picture: The program director presents an overview. He begins by saying that the young people for whom this program was designed changed the program's name within the first six months of its existence. "Don't call us youth at risk; we are youth who are turning," they insisted, *Uth Turn*. Their new name is their very own, and they can tell you just how true it is.

The director quotes appalling statistics for those in prison in the United States; he tells about programs available on either side of the bars. He quotes the late James Washington, "We are an Easter people living in a Good Friday world." Then he calls forward all the NYTS students, as well as the young people who are part of *Uth Turn*. Before our very eyes, they hold "a feeling session."

"I'm feeling sleepy," one kid admits. A seminarian talks about his frustration, another tells how he discovered kids living in an abandoned building. "This [program] has you doing things with people and reaching for goals you never thought you'd achieve," another seminarian confesses. "But then you achieve them," she adds.

A Korean student apologizes for his limited English and then proceeds to give an extremely poignant and clear description of his fieldwork congregation's inadequacy: "They have a lot of program," he says, shrugging. "Talking, talking, talking; praying, praying, praying." Laughter rings out and he receives a round of applause. The applause comes again, loud, as if at curtain call, when another voice says, "These kids don't have a problem; the problem is with us." Appealing, quiet smiles appear on the young people's faces when they hear someone else declare, "These kids are turning *our* lives around."

Prayer begins with songs that were written by a remarkable man when he was in prison — and after he had been denied parole. Since the man's release, he has come to serve as a congregational youth minister and facilitator with *Uth Turn*. These are songs of hope, songs of faith. We stand. We are called to stand by lyrics that echo Galatians and Ephesians. We hold hands, getting ourselves next to each other for the sake of body as well as mind. The circle crackles with energy; around the circle each offers a word of prayer. There seem to be at least a million dreams, articulated in many accents, spoken in many tones of voice. All human emotion is expressed in these words. I come away knowing I have been held, and feeling like the stars themselves have been rearranged.

Within hours, of course, the other stuff of my world has returned to consciousness, and a lot of it is not good news. But the morning has turned my heart around. As with my experience of a good Virginia reel, after the dance, I feel that I have been swirled about in the midst of a panoply of colors and movement and sound. Surely, if good square dancing can linger in my memory all these years, the hope engendered by such a community can last long enough for me to get a better grasp on Philippians 1:6 ("I am confident that the one who began a good work in you will bring it to completion at the day of Jesus Christ"). What the seminarian said about the youth, I can say about our students: They turn my life around.

When I first learned about the project out of which this book grew, my imagination led me to music from *The King and I*. In my mind I could hear Anna singing, "It made me think we might be similarly occupied. Shall we dance?"

"Similarly occupied," swirling in color and movement and sound, theological education of all sorts taking place on the North American continent. What a wondrous venture, what an amazing dance in the divine design. The very thought of all the turning, and re-turning, and turning around of hearts and minds and ministries, turns me around as well.

This *turning* is the whole point of the only two-volume document in the New Testament: Luke-Acts. From the opening announcement to Zechariah of Elizabeth's conception, to the abrupt close with Paul under house arrest in Rome, Luke's story is one of *turning* the world from darkness to light, from enmity to peace, from brokenness to wholeness — all by the power of the Holy Spirit. The divine breath enters the story before Elizabeth ever bears the Baptist; and it is on Paul's lips at the end of Acts. Luke intends the ending to be abrupt; he seems certain that life in the Holy Spirit will be the way of God's people forever. And Paul in Rome is as good a place as any to stop telling his story.

"When the last little star has left the sky, will we still be together?" Anna sings to the King of Siam. The last little star in God's *oikonomia* is in God's hands. In the meantime, each of us is living the next, yet-to-be-written chapter of Acts, holding fast to God's promise that God will complete our good work. Shall we therefore, even upon bridges, dance?

Questions for Reflection

1. Are we still free? Where are we enslaved by our own ways?

2. Just who are we, anyway? Who is not here?

3. Where is the deep structure? What is really going on here?

4. What trolls and temptations lie beneath the bridge? What is it that causes us to stumble in our mission?

5. In what ways are we, as this body, walking within God's *oikonomia*, divine design? How might we better effect the exchange of energy that is called by the name *reconciliation*?

Part Two

ISSUES IN FORMATION

Seven

Why the Seminary?

A Historical Inquiry

GLENN MILLER

As this present volume makes clear, Christian denominations today prepare candidates for the vocation of ministry in a variety of ways. Yet, for most American religious bodies, the graduate professional school, or seminary,[1] remains the preferred method of preparation, and graduation from such an institution is either recommended, or required, for ordination (or for full ministerial standing). Even where historically this has not been the norm, as is true of many charismatic denominations, church leaders today have begun to establish theological schools similar to those maintained by other Protestant groups. However else ministers may be prepared, the seminary continues to play a central role. Perhaps more important, the seminary tends to dictate what is expected in our preparation for ministry. In fact, the curricula of many "alternative" forms of theological education often mirror the standard seminary program. The seminary remains the yardstick by which others are measured. Despite the seeming dominance of the seminary, however, questions about theological education abound.

Mainstream American Protestantism (long the central religious tradition in America) has been in decline for several decades, and these churches are facing serious issues of organization, funding, and mission. Certain issues are quite pragmatic and financial. For example, as congregations become smaller, can they afford to pay the salary of a full-time pastor, a pastor who has invested heavily in seven years of education and who often is saddled with substantial debt for that training? Other questions reach well beyond financial concerns. Theologian Charles Wood notes that what many Americans expect from their pastors differs markedly

117

from what seminary faculties or denominational administrators expect from theological students:

> What the future priests and ministers...need most, in this view, is not objective knowledge of the Christian tradition, not professional skill in the performance of the duties of leadership — though the relative importance of both of these need not be denied — but rather a thorough self-knowledge and self-possession as Christians. Church leaders need not be saints, but they need to be persons who truly understand themselves in the light of the Gospel, and who are able to nurture a similar self-understanding in others.[2]

Are graduate professional schools the best place to inspire "a thorough self-knowledge and self-possession as Christians"? Or is a great deal of what the seminaries do, valuable as it might be from an abstract or scholarly perspective, largely beside the point with regard to the central task of preparing effective church leaders? In other words: *Why the seminary?*

The Power of Tradition

The earliest Christian churches selected leaders from among those persons who had demonstrated that they had gifts in leadership. Certainly these Christian leaders had more education than most of their fellow believers, an education that usually included the ability to read and write easily. (This was especially true after Constantine's fourth-century establishment of Christianity.) But very few Christian leaders had undergone any specific preparation for ministry. Even great intellectuals, such as Augustine, Ambrose, and Jerome, completed only the level of learning expected of all Roman gentlemen. The truth is that early Christian leaders relied upon *secular* knowledge when going about their various *ecclesiastical* duties. There was, as yet, no such thing as a specifically theological education for Christians. Thus, even Scripture and tradition had to be interpreted in accordance with a minimal secular education.

By the time of the early Middle Ages, prospective priests, and especially prospective bishops, were urged to spend time in a monastery (or with a noted bishop) as preparation for their future vocations. In the eleventh and twelfth centuries, the growth of cities contributed to the establishment of universities, places of general study that educated leaders for diverse professions in both church and state. For those who aspired to be bishops, church bureaucrats, or canon lawyers, the university offered an educational path that was an alternative to studying either in a monastery or under the mentorship of a bishop. The mendicant monastic orders, whose mission involved preaching in urban settings, provided the majority of teachers and students in the theological schools that came to be established within universities.

The Protestant Reformation occurred in the midst of a major upheaval in human learning. Printing, which originated in Germany and spread rapidly throughout Europe, had already transformed bookmaking.[3] Using the new technology, a printer now could produce a large run of books that were identical in every respect. Printers ransacked antiquity, searching for materials that they could print and sell on the open market. They encouraged scholars to prepare critical editions that would both compare different manuscripts of the Bible and also suggest a standard text. Nor was newer thought neglected. Scholars, such as Erasmus, became best-selling authors; many found part-time employment as proofreaders and editors.

The Protestant Reformers discovered the new technology to be a crucial and effective weapon in their theological battles with Rome. They produced large quantities of printed materials, including treatises, broadsides, and popular pamphlets.

Education also was profoundly affected by print technology. Led by such reformers of university education as Melanchthon himself, Lutherans adopted the university as their standard of education for the ministry. Within a century, most German pastors had met the new mark. Reformed leaders on the European Continent adopted similar standards.

British reformers took a different tack. Renaissance humanism had an enormous impact on most of the European universities, but especially on Oxford and Cambridge, both of which restructured their programs around the new knowledge.[4] After the Elizabethan settlement, the English church soon replaced the standard of monastic education for clergy with a classical university education. In accordance with her nonreligious, purely political concerns, Elizabeth I envisioned the Anglican pastor as a person of letters, intellectually prepared to take his place next to the squire as a member of the ruling class. Thus, even university study of theology gradually declined, and the new liberal arts program, based on the Latin and Greek classics, became the accepted norm for ordination.

Both the Continental and the English traditions of university education have had a powerful effect on the United States. When the Puritans emigrated to the New World, they quickly established liberal arts colleges on the English pattern. Throughout the nineteenth century, even after the rise of the seminary movement, denominations with British roots argued for the importance of *college* as the cornerstone of a sound preparation for the sacred desk. As these same denominations spread across the American continent, they established liberal arts colleges wherever possible.[5] Only later were seminaries established, either when finances permitted, or in response to theological battles.

On the other hand, Continental Lutherans and the Reformed churches were more enamored of university theology departments than they were of the liberal arts approach.

At first, American Protestants in the Lutheran and Reformed traditions relied heavily on pastors who had received traditional European training. These denominations established their own institutions for educating clergy only when European pastors were no longer available, or when church members became so Americanized that they began to call for pastors who had been born in this country. Whereas Lutheran and Reformed churches often did follow the British-American pattern of college plus seminary, they tended to *interpret* that pattern as a continuation of the European gymnasium (undergraduate) plus university (graduate) education. Throughout American history, the Lutheran and Reformed denominations have had a consistently high percentage of college and seminary graduates with some Lutheran and Reformed bodies attaining almost 100 percent college and seminary completion by their clergy.

Why the seminary? To many Americans, seminaries seem simply to be part of their inherited religious tradition. Religious affiliation often survives longer as a mark of ethnicity than do other aspects of a culture, including food and language. Similarly persistent in its survival is the notion of what constitutes proper education for ministers. No matter how American seminaries might differ from their European antecedents, many Americans have appreciated seminaries as visible signs of continuity with their Protestant past. Seminaries are part of how it always was, and, hence, they have become a *comfortable* part of the present.

The Challenge of a New Nation

If Americans have often felt strong ties with their ethnic homelands, they have also been keenly aware of living in a "new order in time." In no area of American life has this been more evident than in the religious arena.

Following the Revolutionary War, Americans boldly separated church and state. Even though many states quickly adapted corporation law to allow congregations and denominations some measure of legal immortality, churches soon became voluntary associations, accountable only to their own members. Now a person had ecclesiastical status only by virtue of his willingness to attend a given church and to support it financially.

Lacking state support, American churches were forced to *attract* their membership (and their financial base) anew each generation. In a very real sense, therefore, religion became a *commodity* that was subject to market conditions, a commodity that had to be presented as winningly as possible.[6]

What's more, early nineteenth-century culture actually encouraged the new, entrepreneurial style of religion. Sensing a need for religious institutions within their communities, church leaders often acted to satisfy a demand without waiting for any formal ecclesiastical approval. Circuit riders, Baptist farmer-preachers, and colporteurs (i.e., persons who evangelize by means of distributing religious literature) crisscrossed the nation, seeking converts, establishing congregations, and forming new patterns of religious association. In some cases, these democratic ministers were people of true spiritual and religious nobility, who sacrificed their own prosperity in order to bring a healing word to their neighbors. But others had more in common with the then-commonplace patent-medicine salesmen, who hawked their wares to an uneducated and unsuspecting people. To denominational hierarchies, education seemed to be one way to mitigate these unfortunate excesses. Across the boards, church leaders sensed a need to require education for their clergy. Furthermore, every denomination had its core reformers who sought to improve the standards of professional ministry by means of education.

The freestanding seminary, independent of university association, was ideally suited to American free-market religion. The outstanding mark of the seminary was this: *It was a private institution committed to a public task.* Unlike liberal arts schools, seminaries could, and did, adopt theological and ecclesiastical positions that appeal only to a small segment of the population.

During the first half of the nineteenth century, American churches were engaged in fervent theological discourse. The larger denominations were marked by intrachurch theological disputes that were often as passionate as — or even more passionate than — debates that took place across denominational boundaries. In such an environment, seminaries became intellectual citadels of divergent dogmas; often they were geographically placed near the center of a population espousing a strong but controversial theological point of view. Skilled dialecticians, armed with Scripture and syllogism, staffed the seminaries. Andover, for instance, represented "The New England Theology"; Princeton, "Old School Calvinism"; Union, "New School Calvinism"; and Oberlin, "perfectionism." Various new emphases also entered through the seminary gates. For example, in its early days, General Seminary (Episcopal), located in New York City, followed an Anglo-Catholic style. Over time, however, General shifted to the evangelical style of the Oxford movement.[7]

Throughout American history, certain seminaries have maintained a highly ideological character, particularly in the years immediately following their founding. Although in the 1950s both Southern Baptists and United Methodists had founded conventional denominational schools, most other schools founded in the twentieth century were established primarily to maintain distinctive theological or denominational positions. In actuality, seminaries have been organized around issues of biblical inerrancy, premillennial dispensationalism, and traditional Wesleyan holiness. Various distinct theological positions have defined many other schools as well. For years, the University of Chicago Divinity School was home to a particular theological position called "Chicago modernism," and this position renewed itself over several theological generations. Union Seminary (New York) and Yale in the 1940s and 1950s provided institutional bases for American "neo-orthodoxy." Accurately or not, many Americans continue to identify schools as "liberal," "conservative," or "middle of the road."

Religious convictions and theological points of view are, of course, of great importance to the American religious market. The more passionately people believe in a teaching or a church, the more likely are they to contribute sacrificially to an institution that promises to secure the immortality of their convictions.

Still another current of change has influenced the development of American seminaries. Prior to the 1960s, seminaries operated on comparatively small budgets; they had small administrations and faculties, limited physical plants and libraries. Highly committed faculty worked sacrificially for very low wages; to supplement their incomes, they preached and lectured extensively. Under this scenario, a relatively small financial contribution to a seminary could have a large impact on the parent church and its leadership. Furthermore, denominations looked to their seminaries as a source of expertise. Seminary faculty members often wrote church (Sunday) school literature, prepared pamphlets, and spoke at denominational assemblies and meetings. In addition to denominational work, seminary or seminary-related personnel contributed their leadership to various cooperative Protestant enterprises.

Why the seminary? Because in America, *belief counts.* Americans have been attracted to seminaries precisely because these institutions could, and did, articulate and defend particular doctrines or theological positions. Even if all of us do not support Old School Presbyterianism or pretribulation premillennial dispensationalism, certainly some of us do — and quite passionately at that. In many cases, the seminaries have served as an effective means of promoting and disseminating our most cherished convictions about God, humankind, and the universe.

The Challenge of Modernity

Arthur Schlesinger Sr. has called the period immediately following the Civil War a crucial period for American Protestants.[8] Subsequent research has confirmed his judgment. After the Civil War, three issues confronted the churches: the new biblical criticism, the debate over evolution, and growing urbanization. Each of these issues moved seminaries closer to being the center point of American ministerial preparation.

Nineteenth-century biblical criticism and the theory of evolution represented major intellectual shocks for many Protestants. But even the most astonishing events can be better understood if one searches for the antecedents of these events. The careful historian of Protestant theology can trace the gradual development of modern biblical studies from its origins in the textual studies of Renaissance scholars to late-nineteenth-century scholarship.[9] In such studies, each step toward greater clarity appears to be implicit in the previous one, yet the testimony of contemporaries that some events were revolutionary should not be put aside.

In Europe and America, late-nineteenth-century theologians believed that they faced *new* intellectual difficulties and that these difficulties required serious, careful reflection. If few of these theologians are read today, it may be because they embraced the issues of their own time so completely that when the intellectual issues changed, their writings became dated.

At the same time, the sheer mass of intellectual material, both printed and otherwise, increased almost geometrically. Few scholars could keep up with the increasing pace of discovery and debate. At best, one could keep up with a single discipline or, to be more precise, one segment within a discipline. In response, theological schools, both in Germany and in the United States, promoted increased *specialization* among their faculties. Many academic disciplines divided into subdisciplines. If the churches were to have a serious place in the intellectual life of their times, they had to keep up with the broader intellectual revolution.

Popularization of education signaled that the spiritual and intellectual crisis was not confined to professional theologians or scholars. Urbanization placed a premium on education. The high school, initially a popularized version of the classical academy, quickly became a common middle-class attainment. College and university enrollments grew as an increasingly organized society required more and more highly educated professionals and other leaders. The modern corporation consumed talented leadership as rapidly as it did other natural resources.[10] Moreover, this more educated people began to seek ministers who could speak to them at their own level of education. In short, educated people want their religious leaders and spiritual guides to be at least as well educated as they are. Consequently, many Americans with knowledge of the larger intellectual world eagerly sought pastors, such as Henry Ward Beecher and Harry Emerson Fosdick, who understood their questions (or, at least, were not *afraid* of the questions!). Conservatives too sought informed and convincing spokespeople for their positions.

Churchgoers' desire for intellectual competence in their clergy most certainly increased their commitment to seminaries. In some ways, this caused a paradoxical situation for many critics of the seminary at the turn of the century. William Rainey Harper, the energetic first president of the University of Chicago, made sweeping indictments of the inherited seminary in his article "Shall the Theological Curriculum Be Modified, and How?"[11] As he saw it, these schools were devoted to an arcane curriculum, to outmoded methods of instruction, and to a form of intellectual inquiry that simply omitted modern physical and social science. As Harper saw it, seminaries were dated institutions serving a dying social institution. But Harper did not draw the further, and perhaps obvious, conclusion — that is, he did not advocate the abolition of the seminary. The moral and religious problems posed by modernity pressed in upon church leaders, especially upon those who refused to allow themselves or their seminaries to sink into irrelevance. In other words, the schools' very weakness in light of modern conditions pointed to the importance of such institutions — if the schools could in fact be brought up to date.

At the turn of the twentieth century, American popular religion also deeply influenced the seminary. In the antebellum period, the Baptists, Methodists, and Disciples of Christ challenged the dominance of various established traditions, such as the Lutheran, Reformed, and Anglican churches. The Baptist, Methodist, and Disciples of Christ churches won significant numbers of adherents because of (1) aggressive evangelism, (2) having ministers who came from the same social class as their church members, and (3) an aggressive Americanism coupled with democratic ideology. But by 1870, social changes among the membership of these denominations — particularly the migration of significant numbers of people to urban centers — created a demand for a more adequately trained leadership.

A number of schools were established in response to these social changes — schools that duplicated existing seminaries in many ways. However, the *popular* genius of these denominations deeply influenced their styles of education. In a survey of theological education published in 1924, Robert Kelly noted that schools related to the Baptist, Methodist, and Disciples denominations placed major emphasis on practical theology, especially on such areas as religious education and social ethics.[12] Shailer Mathews of Baptist University of Chicago spoke openly of the way in which these particular seminaries improved the "efficiency" of the ministry.

This ascendancy of practical theology also influenced schools related to the Congregational, Presbyterian, and Episcopal churches. Congregationalist seminaries were quite open to including these new disciplines, whereas Presbyterian and Episcopal schools often resisted their inclusion in an academic curriculum. At Presbyterian-related Princeton, for example, student demands for more courses in religious education almost toppled the presidency of Francis Patton, and these demands were a major factor in the school's transformation under President J. Ross Stevenson in the 1920s.[13] In response to similar demands, Union Theological Seminary in New York City called a Methodist, George Coe, to head its new department of practical theology. The same school called another Methodist, Harry F. Ward, to teach social ethics. Whether resisted or embraced, the newly instituted disciplines were there to stay. Although their position and valuation in seminary curricula has varied greatly since the 1920s, courses in practical theology have never disappeared.

Why the seminary? Seminaries seem to be the best way to deal with the problem of *relevance,* both intellectual and social. Although studying theology privately has always been difficult, the theological and ecclesiastical issues that emerged in the late nineteenth century made "knowledge instructors" even more crucial. To master the newer approaches to biblical criticism, students and teachers needed much more than a dab of Greek and a dash of Hebrew, and any significant discussion of the theory of evolution demanded great sensitivity to the rather complex philosophical issues of transcendence and process. Furthermore, our changing social order posed numerous ethical difficulties. In response to modernity, seminaries added faculty members and increased their library holdings. The money to pay for these improvements was generated by industrial prosperity, but the will to carry out needed changes appears to have come from the theological situation.

Wars, Rumors of War, and the Depression

Wars often mark significant transitions in a nation's history, which was particularly true of the United States from 1910 to 1960. During this period, the United States participated in two world wars; we developed, advocated, and exported some of the most savage weapons of mass destruction known to humanity; and we engaged in global confrontation with the Soviet Union. Even brief intervals of peace were dominated by international tension. During the 1930s, pacifism was the dominant ethical issue debated in colleges and seminaries. Yet, at the end of the decade, "realist" theologians had reached two conclusions: Nazi Germany had to be stopped at all costs, and war with Japan was all but inevitable.[14] The 1950s were bookended by Asian wars, both of which were fought in the shadow of the Cold War with the Soviet Union. The deployment of atomic and hydrogen bombs also cast a pall over a seemingly placid decade.

During these same years, 1910–60, the nation experienced one of its most dramatic cycles of boom and bust. Reaching unprecedented heights in the 1920s and equally unprecedented lows in the 1930s, the American economy rebounded with the advent of World War II. At the nadir of the Depression, even the Rockefellers had to curtail their expansive philanthropy. Money simply was not to be had.

Hard times and war accelerated the mass movement of people to cities and suburbs — the metropolises. Rural areas found themselves drained of young people and also drained of hope. The population shift was particularly significant for America's Protestant denominations, which predominantly comprised rural and small-town churches. Not surprisingly, many seminaries developed programs aimed at cultivating effective rural-church ministers. Some schools advocated nontraditional solutions to the problems facing country churches, one such solution being the consolidation of congregations.

Americans learned many things from the experience of war and depression. From the jumble of alphabet agencies that, in the 1930s and 1940s, were created to deal with various crises came what was to be perhaps the primary lesson learned by Americans: organize! American faith in organizations, and in the experts who ran them, was never higher than in the 1940s. If an organization failed — and many of President Franklin Roosevelt's most prized experiments died very quickly — it was replaced by a new organization that learned from the mistakes of the old. The churches, of course, lacked the resources needed to play the organizational game in earnest, but they accepted the belief that cooperation would permit them to be once again the "soul of the nation." Ecumenism, therefore, became the wave of the future.

America's entry into World War I placed a heavy burden on the seminaries, most of which were small institutions with fewer than one hundred students (some with considerably fewer). Enrollments decreased dramatically because of Selective Service and the various Armed Forces' recruiting campaigns. In 1918 leaders from the Baptist seminaries met to discuss their common problems; this meeting inspired President Lowell of Harvard University to call for a Conference of Theological Seminaries in 1919. As was true of many future ecumenical meetings, the primary result of this gathering was the decision to form a continuing committee. The conference brought together seminary leaders to exchange information about common concerns. But, most importantly, the conference identified a community of expertise that transcended denominational boundaries.

War did more than suggest organization. At the beginning of World War I, the U.S. government had no plan for providing ministry to members of the Armed Forces. The relatively new Federal Council of Churches sponsored a committee that met periodically to deal with questions related to qualifications for military chaplains. In addition, the committee faced the difficult task of coordinating an unwieldy confederacy of organizations, a confederacy from which its members were drawn. Perhaps the committee's most important discovery was how difficult it was to determine the eligibility of clergy for chaplain's commissions.[15] World War I ended before ever this issue could be settled, but by the time of World War II, the Association of Theological Schools (ATS) had proposed that the bachelor of divinity degree be recognized as the standard qualification for military chaplains. Seminaries gained immense prestige from the government's acceptance of this standard.

The passion for organization that marked these decades was reflected in three notable seminary surveys: Kelly, Brown-May, and Niebuhr-Williams-Gustafson.[16] Like all historical records, these surveys are subject to a number of different interpretations. At a minimum, they tell the story of the seminary's progressive ascendancy. At the time of Kelly's 1924 survey and of the Brown-May survey almost a decade later, approximately one-third of American mainline ministers were educated in both college and seminary. But many of those with seminary training did not have the prerequisite college background. The most common theological degree was the bachelor of divinity, awarded in most cases after completion of both college and seminary. Yet many schools offered the bachelor of theology degree, which combined two years of liberal arts (primarily English and languages) with a three-year program in theology.

By 1957, when the Niebuhr-Williams-Gustafson survey was published, the situation had changed utterly. Successful completion of both college and seminary was now the norm. The Baptist and Methodist Churches were on the verge of requiring the bachelor of divinity for ordination.

The Brown-May study, published in 1934, was a particularly important step in the acceptance of the BD degree as a prerequisite for ordination. Rockefeller's Institute of Social and Religious Research agreed to finance the Brown-May study, if the seminaries would agree to use the study's findings as an impetus for moving towards the establishment of an accrediting agency. The suggestion was a timely one. Many professional schools, including schools of medicine and dentistry, by now had merged with universities. These partnerships stabilized academic standards and provided the professional schools with intellectual credibility. In addition, the university professional schools benefited from the general movement towards regional accreditation. Professional associations and the various state governments also set and maintained standards of knowledge and practice for various occupations. Seminaries, on the other hand, with the exception of a handful of schools related to private universities, were not regulated by these larger standards-generating agencies. If the seminaries were to maintain truly professional standards, they would also have to set, and enforce, such benchmarks.

By 1936 the new American Association of Theological Schools had established minimum standards and had conducted its first investigations of member schools. The fact that initially many schools did not meet all of the association's qualifications was not regarded as disheartening because accreditation tends to improve institutions incrementally, one slow reform at a time. What was important was that the schools were moving in the direction of higher standards. The 1954 Sealantic Grants, the last of John D. Rockefeller's generous gifts to theological education, strengthened the association by providing funds for a paid staff and an office, thus giving the standards further legitimacy.

The Second World War was financed by promises, including the popular war bonds. The most important promise was that the nation would reward those who had served in the Armed Forces. After the war, the G.I. Bill provided substantial educational benefits to returning servicemen and women. Those who might never have had the opportunity to attend college or professional school were now able to enroll — and they did so in large numbers. Seminaries benefited financially from increased enrollments, of course, but they also benefited from the increasingly accepted belief that the completion of both college and seminary was an attainable norm. The G.I. Bill had similar effects on other professions and contributed to the establishment of a large, comparatively prosperous American middle class. Rural southerners, Catholics, and other white Americans who had previously found themselves on the fringes of society now moved closer to the center.

Other veterans' benefits redounded to the seminaries' advantage. Through guaranteed G.I. mortgages, for instance, the government directly and indirectly financed the growth of the suburbs. The government provided indirect support for the new suburban communities, including giving aid to public schools. Interstate highways connecting suburbs to cities were partially financed by the federal government as a defense measure. The creation of suburban communities had several ramifications for the church: the establishment of new congregations, the reestablishment of many almost-defunct country churches, and available funding for new buildings and additions to older buildings. Whether or not one wants to speak of the postwar years in terms of a religious revival, it is hard to deny that during those years religion became a booming enterprise. More Americans than ever before became affiliated with the church, regularly attending worship services and contributing financially.

American theology in the 1920s and 1930s was dominated by the acrimony of the fundamentalist-modernist controversy. By contrast, the

1940s and 1950s could be called one of the golden ages of American theology. The religious thought of these decades was fed by many springs: the American realist theology of the 1930s, the neoorthodoxy of Barth and Brunner, the Luther renaissance, the worldwide ecumenical movement, the biblical theology movement, existentialism, demythologizing, Catholic neo-Thomism, and the depth psychology movement. Intellectual excitement could be found throughout the curriculum. Teachers of Scripture, for instance, became less concerned with the nuances of critical theory than they had been in earlier decades; the emphasis now was on larger issues of interpretation. An example of this shift in emphasis would be the publication of the Interpreter's Bible by Abingdon Press. Theologians sought new ways to address the contemporary world. Paul Tillich's "method of correlation" was more than a disciplinary guideline; it became the motto of a generation that desperately wanted to find its own Christian voice. Church historians rediscovered the spiritual and theological depth of the Reformation, and the study of American religious institutions became an accepted part of the seminary curriculum.

Why the seminary? The seminary fit the needs of two generations of twentieth-century Americans. From 1910 to 1960, the seminary was in harmony with the deeper course of American life. For the generation that fought the Second World War and that held political, economic, and social power through the 1980s, the seminary was part of the postwar revival, part of the movement to make America "what it ought to be." The schools and the ministers they produced were associated with American church history's largest religious boom and with some of its most profound religious thought. If this era later resulted in nostalgia among people of the postwar generation, at the time it released considerable religious energy.

A Bridge over Troubled Waters

The seminary movement reached an apparent high point in the 1960s and early 1970s. Many evangelical or conservative theological schools adjusted their programs, often eliminating flourishing bachelor of theology programs, and sought accreditation from the American Association of Theological Schools. As Pentecostal and holiness churches have prospered and founded their own schools, they have often done so after consultation with officials of the Association of Theological Schools.

An extremely significant movement in the life of the American seminary has been the transformation of the Roman Catholic seminary. I remember the excitement when Jesuit Woodstock Seminary took up residence on Morningside Heights and coordinated its program with that of Union Seminary (New York). The cooperation between these two schools represented an important milestone. More important yet was the gradual movement of Roman Catholic schools toward incorporating modern scholarly disciplines and professional ministerial studies into their curricula. Present-day Roman Catholic seminaries often are very different institutions than were their predecessors. Protestant schools, likewise, have changed as a result of cross-fertilization with Roman Catholic seminaries. Interestingly, Jewish Theological Seminary in New York, while continuing to teach traditional Jewish content, has adopted many of the standards common to other theological schools and has even associated itself with the Association of Theological Schools, although not as a full member.

The program of the Association of Theological Schools has also reflected its success in establishing minimum standards for seminaries. Retaining its important role in accreditation, the association has expanded the number and quality of member services. *Theological Education,* the association's journal, has matured into a professional journal that focuses on both religious and educational issues. In addition, the association has sponsored important programs on issues of concern to member schools.

Yet, for all the financial prosperity of the last forty years, certain factors have eroded the seminaries. As American higher education has become organizationally more complex, theological schools have followed suit. Much of this growth in complexity has been involuntary. Schools struggling to meet both regional and ATS accreditation standards have had to expand staff. Other issues, too, have demanded administrative answers. Traditionally, denominational seminaries recruited many of their students from a network of colleges. The denominational colleges, or at least their religion or Bible departments, sought to nurture the students' interest in religious vocations, and then to direct interested young people towards particular seminaries. These networks, however, have weakened and declined. As a result, seminaries have had to invest more funds in recruiting beyond denominational borders. Furthermore, because the average age of seminarians has increased, the schools often have had to promote themselves to a much wider population base.

Perhaps most seriously, the seminary's position in the academic study of religion has changed. At the end of the Second World War, many educators became convinced that colleges and universities ought to expand course offerings that supported basic Western values. One result of this conviction was the inauguration, or strengthening, of religion departments. The Supreme Court, often responsive to public opinion, legitimated these efforts by drawing a careful distinction between teaching *about religion* and teaching *religious practices*. The first was constitutional; the second was not. College and university religion professors quickly embraced the new canon and expanded their course offerings. In 1963 the National Association of Biblical Instructors was renamed the American Academy of Religion (AAR), and by the 1990s the AAR was attracting more than five thousand people to its annual meetings.[17]

The AAR has had considerable impact on the seminaries. If nothing else, the expansion of college and university work in religion provided more employment opportunities for persons with advanced degrees in theological and religious studies. But this same expansion of employment opportunities also served to change the reference community for seminary faculty. Before the 1960s, seminary faculty salaries and workloads were usually compared to those of small denominational colleges; salaries and workloads were now compared with those of the larger academic world. Positions that seemed highly privileged a few years earlier no longer seemed so privileged.

College and university religion departments, of course, existed within much larger institutions, which set elaborate standards for faculty promotion, retention, and tenure. Naturally, those who taught in religion departments were expected to meet the same standards as did their secular colleagues. Many papers presented at AAR meetings, for instance, were drafts of publications designed to help a professor win the prize of a fully tenured position. As the prestige of college, and particularly university, positions increased, seminary faculties sought to receive the same protections (i.e., tenure) and to meet the same standards as those found in colleges and universities. For some time, university divinity schools had adhered to these standards, which gradually became a component of nearly every seminary program. What it meant to be a seminary faculty member changed utterly in response to the new expectations.

To be sure, seminary faculties always included persons engaged in serious scholarly research, and many seminary professors were renowned for their publications. Few contemporary scholars could assemble the impressive publication records of such nineteenth-century figures as Charles

Hodge or Benjamin Warfield. But much nineteenth- and early twentieth-century publication was focused on contemporary ecclesiastical issues. Even in such specialized areas as biblical studies, many seminary teachers worked as earnestly on practical studies as they did on their specific areas of research. The new university standards, in effect, narrowed the field of professorial interest to purely academic questions. Whether this change *improved* the intellectual standards of the seminaries or not, it *did* make those standards more technical and more oriented to the larger scholarly world.

Many early members of college and university religion departments were educated in Protestant seminaries and, in fact, taught a secularized version of Protestant theology. But, over time, seminaries lost their dominant position as the training ground for the next generation of university teachers of religious studies. Beginning in the 1960s, it became fashionable for universities with divinity schools (such as Harvard, Yale, and Duke) to separate graduate religious departments from divinity schools, even though these two departments continued to share many of the same personnel. This separation served to legitimate graduate religious studies as a field in which a person could earn a PhD degree; graduate religious studies could no longer be regarded simply as education for a profession. But the separation also marked a gradual shift in advanced training for college and university teaching — a shift away from the seminaries and toward the establishment of religion departments. Seminaries tried to stem the tide by offering a variety of scholarly master of arts or master of theological studies programs that were designed to prepare people for doctoral studies. Although a handful of men and women seeking a college-level teaching career in religious studies have taken advantage of the seminary-based MA and MT programs, many more students have completed their preliminary work in universities or in university-related divinity schools.

Since the civil rights movement of the 1950s and 1960s, Americans have gradually altered their understanding of race and gender; women and members of minority groups have entered occupations previously restricted to white men. In response to these attitudinal and perceptual changes, seminaries have diversified their faculties, initiated departments of African American Studies and Women's Studies, and have recruited women and minority students. In some seminaries, more than 50 percent of the students are female (although faculties have not diversified proportionately). Anxious and sometimes bitter debate has resulted from the seminary's attempt to define its place in a rapidly transforming America.

In addition, seminaries have had to deal with the changing role of religion in American life. Since Vatican II, Roman Catholics have witnessed a decline in new vocations for the priesthood and an even more dramatic decline in new vocations for women's religious orders. The restriction of the priesthood to celibate males has made it difficult for Roman Catholic seminaries to compensate for the decline in vocational interest among young men by enrolling older students and women — as in fact Protestant schools have done.

Among Protestants, the changing role of religion has been experienced in ways both similar to and different from the Roman Catholic experience. During the past two decades, mainstream Protestant congregations not only have declined in numbers, but also have aged in comparison to the larger population. Compared to the 1950s, there are far fewer churches of a thousand members or more, far fewer churches with significant disposable income and/or active programs for youth and college students. Perhaps equally serious, although less visible, is the rapid population decline in rural areas, where the majority of Protestant congregations are still located.

As in the Roman Catholic Church, in Protestantism the number of young men interested in ministry has declined precipitously since the end of the Vietnam War. Whereas seminaries have often consciously decided to admit women and older students, the declining number of male candidates has also greatly encouraged such admissions. Student demographics have occasioned other changes. For instance, schools have become far less residential, with more and more commuter students. Lost, in large part, is the informal training that takes place when people who have made similar vocational and religious choices live together.

But the most pressing problem for seminaries since 1960 has been financial. School budgets have risen exponentially, and tuition fees risen proportionately. In some ways, the federal government has unwittingly contributed to the seminaries' financial difficulties by making low-interest loans available to students. This wide availability of borrowed funds has enabled schools to pass on increasing costs to students. However, in a world in which ministerial salaries are still very low — and even declining in proportion to other occupations — passing on costs to students has not been a completely successful tactic, and, in fact, has made the recruitment of ministerial candidates even more difficult. In the 1980s, the Lilly Endowment launched a major initiative to expedite the use of modern fund-raising techniques by seminaries. A number of institutions were helped by this initiative, but the systemic problem remains.

A general sense of crisis and religious decline has had its effect on even the most prosperous of seminaries. The most common answer to the question *Why the seminary?* is that these schools promote strong and healthy churches with vigorous and intelligent leadership. But does this statement also imply its opposite? That is to say, when churches, particularly those richly blessed with schools and teachers, are doing badly, is it because the seminaries are not doing a good job of preparing the leadership? During the 1980s, such prominent scholars as David Kelley and Edward Farley conducted an extensive debate over what made theological education theological. The debate reflected a widespread uneasiness about the seminaries' understanding of their own work. Even if none of the answers to the question has won universal acceptance, the very posing of such a question is significant.

Not surprisingly, the current situation has also led some people to suggest alternative ways of preparing ministers. After all, the ascendancy of the seminary is only one or two generations deep, and neither the American Baptists nor the Methodists, who established their requirements for seminary education late, has been able to provide all their churches with seminary-educated pastors. The Methodist Church has continued its excellent Course of Study program for those who are unable to attend seminary, and it has also maintained quality summer programs for lay pastors. American Baptists often have ignored their own rules and accepted less rigorous standards for ministerial preparation. Southern Baptists and many other evangelicals have never made seminary or college a requirement for service. Particularly in rural areas not served by seminaries, Presbyterian, United Church of Christ, and Lutheran bodies have experimented with judicatory-based theological education. Episcopalians have shown much interest in programs that draw upon the historic relationship of the bishop to congregations in educating new leaders. Catholics are experimenting with parish administrators, permanent deacons, and various other forms of ministry.

Why the seminary? At the end of the past forty years — a period of rapid and thoroughgoing change — the answer to this question may not be as self-evident as it once was. Despite their apparent health, our seminaries today confront deep problems that defy easy solutions: rising costs, high tuition, growing intellectual dependence on the larger academy. And yet, all this does not mean that the seminary is an endangered species. In fact, seminaries are among the best-endowed American religious institutions, and in many cases, they are stronger financially than their sponsoring denominations. The schools also continue to enjoy considerable prestige. Yet, the past forty years spent bridging troubled waters have taken an enormous toll on seminaries. We may have arrived at a time when the question *Why the Seminary?* must, of necessity, be asked in a new way.

Notes

1. The terminology of American theological education implies more diversity than actually exists. In this chapter, the word "seminary" refers to all graduate-level professional schools that prepare people for ministry. Although a handful of these schools are related to universities, most are freestanding institutions with their own faculties, libraries, buildings, and endowments.

2. Charles Wood, "Theological Inquiry and Theological Education," *Theological Education* (Spring 1985): 79.

3. See Elizabeth L. Eisenstein, *The Printing Press as an Agent of Change* (Cambridge: Cambridge University Press, 1979).

4. Mark Curtis, *Oxford and Cambridge in Transition, 1558–1642: An Essay on Changing Relations between the English Universities and English Society* (Oxford: Clarendon Press, 1959).

5. For a classic expression of the rhetoric that united church and college, see Albert Barnes, *Plea in Behalf of Western Colleges: A Discourse Delivered before the Society for Promoting Collegiate and Theological Education at the West,* October 29, 1845 (Philadelphia: William Sloanaker, 1846).

6. R. Laurence Moore, in *Selling God: American Religion in the Marketplace of Culture* (New York: Oxford University Press, 1994), developed this theme as it relates to much of American "popular" culture. However, he did not pay sufficient attention to the extent to which all culture in America, including the high culture of the universities and other institutions of higher learning, is largely a commodity that is valued by society as a whole because of its place in the market.

7. For some of the unpleasantness that was associated with this transition, see Nathan Hatch, *The Democratization of American Religion* (New Haven, Conn.: Yale University Press, 1989).

8. Arthur Schlesinger, "A Crucial Period in the History of American Religion," *Massachusetts Historical Society* 45 (October 1932): 523–46. Frequently reprinted.

9. A history of research is frequently included in introductions to the Old and New Testament or in summaries of research on particular topics in biblical studies. The large number of heresy trials, including the trial of Charles A. Briggs, one of America's greatest Hebraists, is indicative of how these issues were regarded at the time. Briggs's trial was covered extensively in both the secular and religious press. See Mark Steven Massa, *Charles A. Briggs and the Crisis of Biblical Criticism* (Minneapolis: Fortress Press, 1990).

10. For more on the education revolution of the late nineteenth century, see Lawrence Cremin, *American Education: The Metropolitan Experience* (New York: Harper and Row, 1988).

11. William Rainey Harper, "Shall the Theological Curriculum Be Modified, and How?" *American Journal of Theology* (1897): 54.

12. Robert Kelly, *Theological Education in America: A Study of One Hundred Sixty-One Theological Schools in the United States and Canada* (New York: George H. Doran, 1924). Kelly, an early and enthusiastic supporter of the ecumenical movement, was very aware of the impact of denominationalism on the seminaries.

13. The Princeton battles of the early twentieth century, of course, involved a great many issues. For a well-written and able discussion of this era, see David B. Calhoun, *Princeton Seminary*, vol. 2: *The Majestic Testimony: 1869–1929* (Edinburgh: Banner of Truth Trust, 1996).

14. Heather Warren, *Theologians of a New World Order: Reinhold Niebuhr and the Christian Realists, 1920–1948* (New York: Oxford University Press, 1997). Warren has identified the men and women around Henry P. van Dusen as the nucleus of an influential group of Protestant thinkers who were deeply concerned and remarkably well-informed about world affairs. Reinhold Niebuhr was only one of these thinkers; the group also included his brother, H. Richard Niebuhr, along with Paul Tillich, Georgia Harkness, and van Dusen himself. Theologically, the group represented many shades of opinion, from the classical liberalism of van Dusen to the cautious appropriation of Barth by H. Richard Niebuhr.

15. John F. Piper, *The American Churches in World War I* (Athens: Ohio University Press, 1985).

16. Kelly, *Theological Education in America;* H. Richard Niebuhr, Daniel Day Williams, and James M. Gustafson, *The Advancement of Theological Education* (New York: Harper, 1957); William Adams Brown and Mark A. May, *The Education of American Ministers*, 4 vols. (New York: Institute of Social and Religious Research, 1934). Both the Brown-May and Niebuhr-Williams-Gustafson studies sought to place theological education in a broad perspective. Hence Brown-May conducted an exhaustive sociological study of the ministry and its place in American society in conjunction with its survey. Niebuhr, Williams, and Gustafson were part of a project that also included H. Richard Niebuhr and Daniel Day Williams: *The Ministry in Historical Perspectives* (New York: Harper and Row, 1956).

17. D. G. Hart, *The University Gets Religion: Religious Studies in American Higher Education* (Baltimore: Johns Hopkins University Press, 1999).

Eight

Education or Calling

*What Makes a Commissioned Lay Pastor
a Pastor?*

KEN MCFAYDEN

*Commissioned lay pastors in the Presbyterian Church (U.S.A.) have
a great deal to offer the church at a time when, for various reasons, a growing number of congregations are unable to employ
seminary-educated clergy. Increasingly, commissioned lay pastors
are serving in congregational ministry positions that historically
have been served by seminary-trained clergy. As a result, the church
has had to face a number of questions, including: What sort of educational preparation does a person need in order to be "fit" for lay
pastoral ministry? In the future, new questions are likely to emerge
as we in the church reflect more broadly upon our theology of ordination, upon our understanding of vocation, and upon the nature
of the office of pastor.*

My participation in the Alternatives in Theological Education Project
has woven together a number of strands in my professional life. For
over five years, while serving as executive director of the North Central Career Development Center in New Brighton, Minnesota, I worked
with people who were either in the process of preparing for a church
vocation or who were already serving in ministry settings as pastors,
educators, chaplains, missionaries, or judicatory staff. Toward the end
of my tenure at the center, I conducted candidacy assessments for persons in two presbyteries within the Presbyterian Church (U.S.A.) who
were preparing to become commissioned lay pastors. The research for
my doctoral dissertation, "Threats to the Formation of Pastoral Identity
in Theological Education," involved a great deal of reading, observation, and reflection upon formation for ministry within the theological

classroom. This research proved to be quite helpful to me in my work at the North Central Career Development Center, where I encountered persons at many different stages on their vocational journeys.

Since March 1998, I have served on the Advisory Board of the Alternatives in Theological Education Project. At a number of consultation meetings, I have heard Lance Barker and Ed Martin present their findings and solicit the input of church leaders who are involved with alternative theological education programs. I learned that these alternative programs have both increased and expanded during the past decade, and that these programs have had significant impact upon the church and its leadership.

When asked to contribute a chapter to this book, my response was enthusiastic. However, I am aware that my perspective is quite limited, and that the narrowness of my experience with alternative theological education programs necessarily influences any contribution I would hope to offer. To be sure, I write out of a number of contexts that shape my perspective when I hear the experiences of others, and when I identify thematic hopes and concerns: I am (a) a white male who was born into a large, predominately white, upper-middle-class Presbyterian congregation in Raleigh, North Carolina; (b) a Presbyterian minister, ordained in 1986, with five years of experience in local church ministry, six years of part-time experience in hospital chaplaincy, and five years of experience in a church career development center; and now (c) a faculty member of a Presbyterian seminary.

Professionally, my contact with commissioned lay pastors (CLPs) in the Presbyterian Church (U.S.A.) has been limited to candidacy assessments and a retreat on leadership effectiveness I led for CLPs and potential CLPs.

Certainly I cannot provide definitive guidance for assessing the role of commissioned lay pastors in the Presbyterian Church (U.S.A.), a denomination in which, during the last two centuries, congregations typically have been served by clergy educated according to the classical model of theological education. Rather I will attempt to offer some defining questions for the church as it continues to examine the need for pastoral leadership, and as it evaluates the degree to which commissioned laypersons may represent an appropriate resource for meeting such needs.[1]

I am aware that any other person who addressed this topic would do so quite differently. Nevertheless, to acknowledge *that* reality does not undermine the validity of my experience and of my reflections upon that experience.

Commissioned Lay Pastors

There follow two stories — composite portraits drawn from the men and women I have encountered in my work with commissioned lay pastors.

Mary describes herself as "a child of the church." She grew up in a family that throughout Mary's childhood and adolescence was quite active in the life of its Presbyterian congregation. Looking back, she has fond memories of pastors who served the congregation during formative years in her life; she valued these pastors as models of piety, kindness, and genuineness. Similarly, her Sunday school teachers and youth choir directors provided significant models of faith, complementing what she learned from her parents. For her, church was a "grace-filled" place that nurtured her faith, her sense of goodness, and her love of other people.

Now in her sixties, Mary smiles as she recounts the limited vocational options that seemed to be available to her as a young adult. From the perspective of her parents and community, she could become a teacher, a nurse, or a wife and mother. Given the positive ways in which she had been influenced by teachers at school and at church, she chose to be an elementary school teacher. Subsequently she married. With the birth of her first child, Mary resigned her teaching position so that she could be a full-time mother. Through the years she became increasingly involved in church, school, and community life. In each of these settings, after her children grew older, she served in a variety of leadership roles. At church Mary taught Sunday school, sang in the choir, and served as an elder. She recalls that other women in the congregation viewed her as someone to whom they could turn for support.

After her children had grown up and after her husband died, Mary felt at loose ends. Community involvement did not bring her as much fulfillment as it had when her children were younger. She found herself wanting something more. Her pastor suggested that she consider enrolling in the presbytery's Lay Academy, a program designed to offer quality theological education for laity and to prepare lay leaders for service as commissioned lay pastors. In Mary, her pastor discerned both a keen desire to learn and a gift for pastoral ministry.

Partly because she had always held pastors in such high esteem, Mary experienced much ambivalence about her own potential for becoming a lay pastor. Nevertheless, led by curiosity, she enrolled in the program.

Soon her ambivalence gave way to gratitude for all that she was learning about the Bible, theology, church history, and pastoral care. Although she did not see herself as "schooled" enough to preach well, her peers and teachers perceived in her a knack for communicating with integrity and liveliness the biblical story.

After completing the Lay Academy in the spring of 1998, Mary was approved by her presbytery's Committee on Ministry, and subsequently she was commissioned as a lay pastor. She now preaches on a weekly basis in a small congregation, and she provides that congregation with the most continuous ministry they have experienced in seven years. Because she has lived for years in a community near the church she serves, many members of the congregation remark that Mary is "one of them."

Unlike Mary, Joseph grew up in a family that, over the course of his childhood and adolescence, was affiliated with a number of different congregations — Presbyterian, Baptist, Methodist, and nondenominational. To his father and mother, denominational affiliation was not very important. What they looked for in a church was a preacher who based sermons on the Bible, a community of believers who lived their faith, and programs for children and youth that would instill appropriate values. When his parents judged that a congregation failed to meet one of these criteria, Joseph's family would move to another church.

Reflecting on his religious upbringing, Joseph observes that he gained a wide perspective with regard to faith formation and development. He identifies the benefits of his religious upbringing to be: (a) deep commitment to a highly personal faith, and an openness to sharing that faith with others; (b) high expectations of the ministry of the church, as represented by the efforts of pastors and laypersons; (c) a number of important models of faith and practice; (d) a rich knowledge of the Bible; and (e) experience of many different denominational traditions. At the same time, he reports that he is likely to become frustrated when others do not meet his high expectations — especially if those people hold formal leadership roles in the life of a congregation.

As an adult, Joseph has long been active in a Presbyterian congregation, serving in a variety of leadership capacities: Sunday school teacher, worship leader, youth group advisor, choir member, elder, trustee, and member of several presbytery committees. Joseph reports that at several points during his life, a number of people have asked him if he ever considered attending seminary — given his gifts, interests, values, and faith commitments. According to Joseph, a seminary education has been, in many ways, a dream and only a dream. In his family of five, he is the sole income earner. He indicates that he never discerned a strong enough call — nor did he possess the necessary financial standing — to justify leaving his employment, relocating his family, and undertaking a three-year seminary program.

Recently retired and enjoying excellent health, Joseph is now seeking ways in which to channel his energies. He wants to do something that can make a difference in the lives of others. When he learned of the commissioned lay pastor training program in his presbytery, he decided to give it a try. After all, the church had always been at the center of his life, and his gifts for ministry had repeatedly been affirmed.

At present Joseph is halfway through the training program. He values the opportunity to deepen his knowledge and to improve his skills for ministry. He is uncertain where this training may lead. He does not feel called to be a pastor, and he often says, "It's all in God's hands, anyway." However, Joseph has a strong desire to serve the church and is keenly aware of the severe shortage of seminary-educated pastors in the rural area in which he lives.

These composite profiles reflect the stories of some of the persons who come to the CLP training programs in order to discern whether or not they have appropriate gifts for serving the church as commissioned lay pastors. Based on interviews and evaluations, I would offer the following general impressions of what people like Joseph and Mary bring to this ministry:

- A deep, abiding sense of the church's heritage;
- A history of active involvement in the life of a congregation, and often in the wider church as well;
- The formation of significant relationships with other persons of faith;
- The support of other people who have urged them to explore a call to commissioned lay pastoral ministry;
- A desire to express their gifts, interests, values, life experience, and faith commitment in meaningful and appropriate ways;
- A clear understanding of the ethos of their local congregations;
- Leadership gifts, which have often been demonstrated in both church and community;

- A wealth of life experience; and

- A motivation to serve that issues from a love for, and commitment to, the church. (In my experience, these folks have not been motivated by the career paradigm that has emerged in many circles of pastoral ministry during the past fifty years.)

Overall, I have been very favorably impressed with the quality of persons who have become (or are in the process of becoming) commissioned lay pastors. Vocationally, their perception of being called to this ministry seems clear, their motivations healthy, and their expectations realistic. Psychologically, they generally bring well-formed personalities to their new vocation. Those with whom I have worked have appeared to be healthy and resilient, possessing psychological resources that would serve them well in the context of lay pastoral ministry.

Questions Raised about Education and/or Training for Commissioned Lay Pastors

Given the gifts that many commissioned lay pastors bring to a vocation in ministry, the church must ask: In order to be "fit" for lay pastoral ministry, what else do these candidates need that they do not already have? What requirements must be satisfied before they are commissioned? For many people in the church hierarchy, any answer to these questions quickly focuses on some degree of *education* that will appropriately prepare laypeople for this form of ministry.

In the Presbyterian Church, as well as in a number of mainline traditions, the master of divinity degree has been the normative degree for persons pursuing a vocation in ordained ministry. With regard to the question of requirements for commissioning CLPs, it may be helpful to examine the program content of the MDiv degree — especially since the traditional seminary curriculum forms the basis of many alternative theological education programs.[2]

When describing the program content of the MDiv degree, the Association of Theological Schools in the United States and Canada identifies four key dimensions. Following each of these four areas, I will pose questions that relate to alternative theological education.

1. *Religious Heritage: The program shall provide structured opportunity to develop a comprehensive and discriminating understanding of the religious heritage. This includes instruction in Scripture, in*

the historical development and contemporary articulation of the doctrinal and theological tradition of the community of faith, and in the social and institutional history of that community.

Questions Regarding Commissioned Lay Pastors: If we are to agree that instruction in Scripture, doctrine, theology, and church history is important for commissioned lay pastoral ministry, how much instruction is appropriate? How might an alternative theological education program determine the desired breadth of material? And how would the program go about accomplishing that instruction? How might a CLP's base of knowledge be measured?

2. *Cultural Context: The program shall provide opportunity to develop an understanding of the cultural realities and structures within which the church lives and carries out its mission. This includes instruction in contemporary cultural and social issues and their significance for ministry, and the global, multicultural, and cross-cultural nature of ministry in North American society.*

Questions Regarding Commissioned Lay Pastors: How important are cultural and social issues in the preparation of CLPs? Given the rapidly changing nature of the church within North American society, what might be some implications for the church if cultural and social issues are *not* adequately addressed in alternative theological education programs?

3. *Personal and Spiritual Formation: The program shall provide opportunities through which the student may grow in personal faith, emotional maturity, moral integrity, and public witness. Ministerial preparation includes concern with the development of capacities — intellectual and affective, individual and corporate, ecclesial and public — that are requisite to a life of pastoral leadership. This includes the provision of opportunities (a) for spiritual, academic, and vocational counseling, (b) for careful reflection on the role of minister as leader, guide, and servant of the faith community, and (c) for developing commitment to Christian faith and life.*

Questions Regarding Commissioned Lay Pastors: Given the attributes that many CLPs bring to their educational preparation, how much attention should the church give to examining the CLP candidates' personal faith, emotional maturity, moral integrity, public witness, and/or commitment to Christian faith and life? (Perhaps this needs to be more of a concern for theological schools than for alternative programs.)

4. *Capacity for Ministerial and Public Leadership: The program shall provide theological reflection on and education for the practice of ministry, in both ecclesial and public contexts. This includes instruction in the areas of ministry practices and educational experiences within supervised ministry settings.*

Questions Regarding Commissioned Lay Pastors: What skills might CLPs need to develop in the areas of preaching and worship leadership, education and nurture, pastoral care, and church administration? How might their skills be evaluated, and by whom? What opportunities might be available for CLPs to work in supervised ministry settings, wherein candidates might receive encouragement, modeling, challenge, and nurture?

General Questions: If our goal is to equip appropriately those persons who are to serve as commissioned lay pastors, in what ways will alternative theological education programs be similar to, and where will they differ from, traditional seminary and divinity school programs? What, if anything, do ordained pastors need to learn that commissioned lay pastors do not? What, if anything, do commissioned lay pastors need to learn that ordained pastors do not?

Concerns Related to Theological Education for Commissioned Lay Pastors

Training programs for commissioned lay pastors continue to evolve in the Presbyterian Church (U.S.A.). A number of concerns emerge as church leaders assess how pastoral leadership will be provided for congregations that are facing a changing church and world situation.[3]

The Concern for an "Orthodox" Ministry

In their desire to maintain an "orthodox" ministry, many Protestant denominations have sought to control, as much as possible, the education of their pastors. This wielding of control has had a significant influence on theological institutions. A number of church leaders have expressed the fear that (a) "theological tutors" would corrupt students with their personal theological biases, and (b) theological students would lose their doctrinal soundness in an increasingly pluralistic environment. In order to shape students' total experience, theological institutions in the nineteenth century developed legally established confessions of faith and introduced seminary residency requirements.

I wonder whether issues of orthodoxy have been of concern to those responsible for designing and implementing alternative theological education programs. For example, does a given program assume that certain doctrinal beliefs will be taught and/or reinforced by the material or by the instructors? Do overseers of the program attempt to assess the orthodoxy of its teachers in order to assure that participants will not be "led astray" during this time of preparation?[4]

The Concern for an Educated Ministry

In the nineteenth century, Protestant theological seminaries flourished, and major denominations placed increasing emphasis upon an educated clergy. But some Protestant church leaders questioned the necessity of a formal theological education. Not only was it difficult for individuals to complete such an education, but the seminary experience often seemed to separate a minister from the practical experience that was perceived as a necessary prerequisite to success as a preacher.[5] Of such concerns about formal theological education, James Fraser writes:

> Questions about educational requirements were always especially disturbing on the frontier where there were never enough college or seminary trained candidates but there were preachers arising out of the revivals claiming the call of the Spirit. Sectional tension and jealousy tended to aggravate the issue. A fair number of westerners did not trust the sort of schooling going on in the "east" because it tended to elevate the clergy beyond the common people, and, even worse, make them dependent on their books and written sermons rather than the movement of the Spirit which was central to the revival experience.[6]

From this description of formal theological education, several dimensions of "the concern for an educated ministry" can be discerned. I wonder how the emergence of alternative programs might relate to these concerns.

First, leaders of the newer evangelical denominations worried about what would become of the masses of people if only college and seminary graduates were ordained. John A. Broadus, one of the leaders of the movement to found Southern Baptist seminaries, called attention to a critical dilemma for Protestant theological education:

I have profound respect for the ministry of the Presbyterian and Episcopal brethren [*sic*]. . . . But if it hadn't been for the great Methodist and great Baptist bodies, and some others like them, who have encouraged men [*sic*] to preach that were destitute of this artificial course of training, what in the world would have become of the masses of people?[7]

A new pattern of theological education began to emerge that attempted to balance the desire for an educated clergy with the pastoral needs of the common person. Baptists, Methodists, Cumberland Presbyterians, and Disciples of Christ employed informal apprenticeships, preacher's institutes, and circuit riding to prepare individuals for pastoral ministry.

Second, the newer denominations were concerned that formal theological education would elevate clergy above the "common people." Their concern was heightened when they discovered that people who were products of apprenticeship systems could neither meet the desired standards, nor could they compete with the clergy of other denominations. Attempting to maintain distinctiveness from the educational methods of the older American denominations, the newer denominations found an answer in college education. Church leaders reasoned that college education allowed persons preparing for ministry to seize the fruits of higher education without losing their dependence on divine inspiration — rather than professional status — as the source of their spiritual power.[8] Of growing importance was the question of what defines a minister: education or calling?

A third concern emerged when demands for more professionally educated ministers came into conflict with the ideal of a minister who depended only on the inspiration of the Holy Spirit. At the heart of this debate was the question of whether pastoral ministry constituted an office or a profession. Some church leaders believed that professionally educated ministers would lose sight of the ministry as an office to which one was called by God; they regarded a minister not so much as a person who exercises skills as someone who witnesses to experience. Other leaders viewed the ministry as a profession, one that called for the best possible education.

In considering ways in which the concern for an educated ministry may have relevance for alternative theological education programs, I would suggest the following questions for further reflection by the church:

1. What does it mean to be "educated for ministry"?

2. What has motivated church leaders to develop alternative theological education programs? (In the nineteenth century, some church leaders expressed concern for "the masses of the people." Perhaps for churches that have relied historically upon seminary-educated clergy, the concern may now be for the masses of unstaffed churches.)

3. How does the evolution of alternative theological education programs reflect the evolving nature of the relationship between clergy and laity in North America?

4. How might the recent emergence of alternative theological education programs reflect a new frontier for mainline denominations in North America?

The Concern for a "Professional" Ministry

In 1899 William Rainey Harper, the first president of the University of Chicago, wrote an important treatise in which he suggested that the church was not attracting the "best and brightest" to serve as its clergy, and that, in fact, the "best and brightest" were entering the professions of law and medicine.[9] He criticized the seminary for remaining intellectually at a standstill since the days of its origin. Perceiving this stasis as a significant dilemma for the church as it moved into the twentieth century, Harper offered several recommendations to strengthen the enterprise of theological education and to provide the church with better-prepared ministers.

First, he suggested that seminary curricula be modified to take into account the contributions of modern psychology and pedagogy. By considering the individual needs and capacities of each student, seminary education not only would become more attractive to persons desiring professional careers, but also would more effectively prepare students to think for themselves in future ministry placements.

Harper further suggested that theological curricula incorporate the present concerns of the society in which students would be ministering.[10] He recommended that theological institutions break out of their isolation by linking their curricula with those of universities. Students would thereby be provided with opportunities to learn in a context with a diversity of perspectives. Such a model, he suggested, might also broaden the purpose of theological institutions from that of preparing persons for one kind of Christian work, that is, preaching. By developing specialized courses of study, seminaries could prepare persons to be pastors, teachers, administrators, medical missionaries, and church musicians.[11] Such modifications, according to Harper, would create a professional ministry comparable to the professions of law and medicine.

Since Harper's ground-shaking work, several significant studies have examined the "inadequacy" of theological education in preparing persons for pastoral ministry. Some of these studies have asserted that, for a number of years, both the number and quality of ministerial candidates have been declining and that many churches are facing a leadership crisis.[12]

Whereas the concern for a professional ministry focused primarily on academic standards in theological education, a second dimension of professional education began to receive attention as the twentieth century progressed. Particularly in the 1960s, the American Association of Theological Schools in the United States and Canada, under the leadership of Charles R. Feilding, made an intensive effort to identify the difficulty experienced by theological institutions as they attempted to prepare students for a practical ministry. Underlying the work of the American Association of Theological Schools was the distressing assumption that "ministry today is generally discontinuous with the preparation provided for it."[13] Theological educators, as well as ministers, had been experiencing a growing dissatisfaction with the graduate school–based professional model of theological education. In 1966 Feilding wrote:

> Theological education does not prepare for ministry; this is the view I have met most commonly. It was expressed by one group of young ministers from several churches who felt that in their experience theological education had been mainly an obstacle course to be run before entering on a ministry with which it had little connection. These men [*sic*] had all done well in their respective seminaries and had been recommended to me as consultants by responsible seminary or church officials. In varying degrees, they regarded themselves as self-educated after graduation. It is only fair to suppose that seminary discipline may have fitted them to continue their own education and inspired them to do so. The problems to which they drew my attention would surprise no one familiar with the normal pressures of the ministry. From deeply troubled people there were the cries for help for which they were unprepared.[14]

A more satisfactory approach to professional education for ministry, Feilding suggested, would define a single task with four related goals:

the acquisition of knowledge, the development of professional skills, personal growth, and a deepening of Christian commitment.[15] He asserted that whereas each of these goals is crucial to ministry, theological education has often overemphasized the acquisition of knowledge to the detriment of the other three goals. The answer to this predicament, Feilding cautioned, is not to suggest that these goals be conceived as subjects to be taught by appropriate professors. Rather, these goals can only be achieved by giving attention to the relationship of the whole educational system to its students and to their own personal goals.[16] In such a paradigm for professional education, *real* learning would not be confused with the development of a good memory, but would be evidenced in fundamental changes in the attitude and behavior of students toward ministry outside of the formal learning environment.[17]

Reflective Comments

As theological education has become increasingly identified with "professional education" over the course of the twentieth century, I perceive that an unintended by-product has been a significant shift in our conceptualization of pastoral ministry from calling to career. With such a shift have come a number of challenges to the church and its leadership, for example, the unhealthy expectations of many who pursue a church vocation, and the number of persons who self-select ministry as a career choice — persons who have little interest in, or understanding of, the churches they may be called to serve.

In recent years, opportunities for, and responsibilities of, commissioned lay pastors have broadened in the Presbyterian Church (U.S.A.). Alternative theological education programs have been designed and implemented to prepare persons for commissioned lay ministry. As a result, an alternative definition of "pastor" has created a new "crisis of leadership." The church has begun to think more carefully about the nature and purpose of pastoral leadership, and the role of theological education in preparing persons for ministry in the church and world.

As theological education embraces its heritage and moves into the future, I anticipate that the three concerns mentioned in this section will continue to shape the identity and function of theological education, whether that education takes place in a seminary environment or in an alternative program designed by a judicatory. Related to these crises are multiple issues that theological education (and theological educators) must increasingly face in seeking to prepare persons for ministry in the church and world: (1) the changing role of mainline denominations in North America in light of chronic membership decline; (2) the realization that an elitist paradigm of professional education does not meet the needs of ethnic communities, which represent a rapidly growing segment of North American religious life; (3) the globalization of theological education as institutions seek to respond to the realities of global interdependence and polarization; and (4) the demand of marginalized persons for the reformation of the content and process of theological education. If theological education is to move away from an elitist paradigm of professional education, it must develop new conceptual frameworks, pedagogical approaches, and organizational patterns, all of which would be attentive to the social, cultural, intellectual, economic, political, and ecclesiastical context in which the church and its leadership both live and learn. Perhaps the proliferation of alternative programs will serve as the catalyst for this important task.

Conclusion

What makes a commissioned lay pastor a pastor? To some, *education* seems to be the key determinant. In this case, subsequent questions would focus on (a) what candidates need to learn, (b) why they need to learn, (c) how they need to learn, and (d) where they need to learn. To others, *calling* seems to be the key determinant. If so, questions arise regarding (a) the nature of a CLP's (inward) call to this form of ministry, and (b) the church's affirmation of that call.

From my perspective, *the church* is the key determinant. The church is the authorizing body that bears responsibility for determining (a) the criteria by which a person's inward call to commissioned lay pastoral ministry will or will not be affirmed, and (b) the appropriate educational preparation for a person who is to engage in pastoral ministry, whether as a Minister of Word and Sacrament or as a commissioned lay pastor. One need only look at the history of the church to see how its concerns about pastoral ministry and leadership have re-formed expectations of how men and women are to prepare adequately for the ministry to which they feel called.

Questions for Reflection

As the church continues to assess both its needs for pastoral leadership and the degree to which commissioned laypersons can be an appropriate resource for meeting such needs, I offer the following questions for further reflection and discussion in light of what I have learned up to this point in my life and work:

Educationally

1. What does it mean to be "educated for ministry"?

2. How will the church determine the ways in which Ministers of Word and Sacrament and commissioned lay pastors ought to be "educated for ministry"? And how will distinctions between these two roles reflect the church's understanding of the uniqueness of each role?

3. Are those who design alternative programs creating a paradigm for the content and process of theological education that is different from that of the seminary? Or do those programs approximate the seminary curriculum — taught in an alternative context?

4. In what ways might alternative theological education programs prompt seminary leaders to reassess the content and process of their various curricula?

Vocationally

5. What defines a minister: *education* or *calling?*

6. How might the emergence of commissioned lay pastors encourage the church to reassess the model of "church professional," a model that has been operative in many settings for several decades?

7. What impact will the use of commissioned lay pastors have upon our theology of ordination, our understanding of vocation, and the "office" of pastor?

8. How does the work of a commissioned lay pastor differ from the function and role of an elder, as defined in the Book of Order of the Presbyterian Church (U.S.A.)?

Ecclesially

9. What hopes does the church have for future utilization of commissioned lay pastors?

10. What might congregations and judicatories gain from the ministry of CLPs? What might congregations and judicatories be sacrificing?

11. In what ways might the ministry of commissioned lay pastors be threatening to seminary-educated ordained persons? Why?

12. If the crisis of "supply and demand" were to change in the future (for example, if congregations began encouraging a greater number of people to attend seminary in preparation for ordination as Ministers of Word and Sacrament), how might we regard the change as a gain for the church? How might we regard it as a loss?

I have offered some of my most pressing questions. I invite you to raise your own questions, and thereby to enliven the life of the church with honest discourse on issues of authentic ministry.

Notes

1. I am aware that the term "commissioned lay pastor" may not be used in other denominations. However, in order to streamline my language, I use the term throughout the chapter to refer to persons who have been authorized to serve in pastoral ministry. A commissioned lay pastor is "an elder of the Presbyterian Church (U.S.A.), who is granted a local commission by the presbytery to lead worship and preach the gospel, watch over the people, and provide for their nurture and service.... An elder who has been commissioned and later ceases to serve in a particular congregation may continue to be listed as available to serve, but is not authorized to perform the functions of a Commissioned Lay Pastor until appointed again to a particular congregation by the presbytery." From *The Constitution of the Presbyterian Church (U.S.A.) Part II: Book of Order, 2000–2001*, G-14.0801a.

2. The following discussion is drawn from the description of the program content of the master of divinity degree in the *Bulletin of the Association of Theological Schools in the United States and Canada*, 43, pt. 1 (1998): 93–95.

3. I identified the following concerns in my doctoral dissertation, where I suggested that in tracing the evolution of Protestant theological education in North America, it is important to recognize that theological institutions have often developed in crisis. In that research, I identified five crises: (a) the crisis of an orthodox ministry; (b) the crisis of an educated ministry; (c) the crisis of a professional ministry; (d) the crisis of fragmentation in theological education; and (e) the crisis of feminism for theological education. Based on my perceptions of alternative theological education programs designed for commissioned lay pastors, I identify the first three of these as having particular relevance for church leaders.

4. The identification of this issue for alternative theological education programs does not assume that theological education in the context of a seminary or divinity school is immune from such concerns. Just because they were concerns two centuries ago does not suggest that they are not concerns of some persons at the present time.

5. James W. Fraser, *Schooling the Preachers: The Development of Protestant Theological Education in the United States, 1740–1875* (Lanham, Md.: University Press of America, 1988), 80.

6. Ibid., 81.

7. Quoted in ibid., 79.

8. Ibid., 100.

9. W. R. Harper, "Shall the Theological Curriculum Be Modified, and How?" *American Journal of Theology* 3, no. 1 (1899): 45–66.

10. Ibid., 48.

11. For a fuller description of a curriculum that would encourage specialization in ministry, see ibid., 56–59.

12. Three classic studies that provide an excellent starting point for those interested in the development of institutional resources, forms of governance, and curricular patterns of theological schools are as follows: Robert L. Kelly, *Theological Education in America: A Study of One Hundred Sixty-One Theological Schools in the United States and Canada* (New York: George H. Doran, 1924); William Adams Brown and Mark A. May, *The Education of American Ministers,* 4 vols. (New York: Institute of Social and Religious Research, 1934); and H. Richard Niebuhr, Daniel Day Williams, and James M. Gustafson, *The Advancement of Theological Education* (New York: Harper, 1957). Since 1957, much attention in the literature of theological education has centered upon the relationship between the theological school and the church and world.

13. Charles R. Feilding, *Education for Ministry* (Dayton, Ohio: American Association of Theological Schools, 1966), 15.

14. Ibid., 31.

15. Feilding discusses each of these goals at length in ibid., 149–72.

16. Ibid., 173.

17. Ibid., 113.

Part Three

RE-IMAGINING
THE FUTURE

Nine

The Small Church

Radical Reformation and Renewal of Ministry

THOMAS RAY

Northern Michigan is a small diocese comprising small congrega-
tions. Reflecting upon the life and experience of such a diocese
is appropriate. It is also important that we admit that smallness
has rarely been seen as a symbol or sign of success. Small congre-
gations have been beaten down and disparaged for decades. Yet
it may be that our God has chosen that which is unappreciated
and demeaned, that which is weak in the eyes of the world, as
the vehicle of renewal, "so that no one might boast in the pres-
ence of God." The little, the small, may be leading us into the next
millennium. This chapter reflects upon how actual congregations
are moving into a renewed, effective, sustainable baptismal min-
istry at the present time. My fourteen years of sharing the life of
the Northern Michigan diocese have brought me to a perspective
about myself and our Episcopal Church that I would never have
dreamed. In my wildest and most radical imagining I would not
have anticipated what has unfolded for us.

Three Things Which Have Grown Old
and Are Cast Down

In order to appreciate what is happening it is important to recognize the
issues we are facing. Let me catalogue the symptoms that I believe are
pressing us to and into renewal. Enumerating the stimuli is necessary in
order to understand our response. The reader may also consider whether
or not the issues affecting Northern Michigan are also the issues affecting
upon your own situation and experience. Our renewal will be of keener
interest to those who face crises similar to ours.

157

1. Fourteen years ago (even today), were I to ask a faithful adult Christian and Episcopalian to list what s/he does as an active Christian, I would be given a list that would likely include altar guild, lectoring, ushering, teaching church school, serving on the vestry, taking communion to the hospital and homebound, or offering the prayers. As noble as these efforts, often called ministries, are they are all in-house, in-church, institutional. Institutions often regard efforts on behalf of the institution more highly than other efforts. The responsibilities listed could be compressed into one to three hours of a typical week. So where does responsibility at home fit in? Home is rarely mentioned. Where does responsibility at work or responsibilities within one's community or neighborhood fit in? They are rarely mentioned. As old things are being made new it will be important to pursue a reform that will authentically integrate our activities in church with our life in the world of home, work, and neighborhood.

2. We proclaim in our public documents that "The Eucharist (is) the principal act of Christian worship on the Lord's Day and other major Feasts." We read in Holy Scripture that Jesus said, "Where two or three are gathered, I am with you." Yet two large dioceses within the Episcopal Church have stated formally and informally that approximately $120,000 of annual income is necessary for a viable congregation. Many congregations are unable to break bread when they desire such nourishment. They do not have enough money to have their own priest and sacramental worship readily available. Their competence must await the arrival of some outsider to join them, to supply for them. Such small congregations are constantly reminded of their inadequacy, not their competence as Christians. In many dioceses the dignity of a congregation is determined by how much money it has and receives. As contradictory as this is, it is true that if you have sufficient annual income you are a parish with your own rector, pay your fair share to the diocese, have four votes at convention, and stand tall. If you are under financial pressure, you will be demoted to an aided parish with three votes. With further financial pressure you will be made a mission with two votes, told to cluster or close or cluster and then close. For many congregations financial discussions are obsessive and little tithe is devoted to the questions of mission or ministry. Survival is the primary issue — and then we wonder why such congregations are not exciting, vibrant, self-confident, energetic, attractive evangelistic communities. Rectors and vicars in small congregations with limited financial resources know that their salary and

benefits often cost 60 percent or even 70 percent of the sacrificial giving of the congregation. I believe this awareness is cruel and destructive to such clergy. Let me quote a similar observation from a study within the Church of England published in 1990 and titled *Faith in the Countryside.* "Within the lifetime of some of the people in this place, the vicar has changed from being the person who distributed money to those who were the chief charge on the community, to now being the chief charge on the community himself!"[1] These clergy are the same clergy who will be underpaid in their retirement.

3. We proclaim with some pride that we carry the threefold orders of historic ministry: priests, deacons, and bishops. Yet few congregations have ever known an authentic deacon. In many dioceses you meet the diocesan bishop every three or four years. Occasionally a priest visits a congregation coming from somewhere else to supply what is missing and unavailable locally. For these congregations the threefold order of ministry has little reality. In a church where deacons are almost nonexistent and bishops are rarely known, priests/rectors (the root meaning of the word "rector" is ruler) have accumulated to themselves an impossible web, a tangled skein of all three orders. Small congregations still struggling to support a rector experience all of this threefold historic ministry in one person who, being in charge, represents apostolic oversight, priestly, and diaconal ministry. In retrospect it is not surprising that we have serious confusion surrounding the identity of the ordained, who have exaggerated expectations laid upon them, and the unordained, who often see themselves as "only laypersons." Unspoken expectations are brutal. Search committees seek an attractive, self-motivated, energetic person who is a master of liturgy, skilled administrator, dynamic preacher, persuasive teacher, sensitive pastor, genius in crisis intervention, relentless visitor in hospital and home, and who also has high visibility and is respected in the community, and brings in the youth. This job description overburdens, isolates, and breaks many rectors. This job description minimizes the responsibilities of the laity. "Don't expect too much from us, we are only laity, we often don't expect much from ourselves." Someone has observed that in terms of authority, dignity, and expectation there is a greater distance perceived between the baptized and the ordained than the distance between the baptized and the unbaptized. To the degree that this observation holds any truth, to that degree we are in deep trouble.

Our Return to Historical and Theological Roots

Whenever we are troubled as Christians and Episcopalians we return to fundamentals. The spiritual taproot that we share as Christians and Episcopalians is the insight, the revelation, and understanding that this world our God has created is a sacramental world, which is why we have sacraments in the church, not because we are different or weird. We have a sacramental worship and spirituality because our world is sacramental. This insight and integration of life and experience drew me and many reading this chapter to and into the Episcopal Church. A sacramental view of life and experience, a sacramental theology, means that the physical and the spiritual are not separate or in conflict as some Christians believe. The physical and the spiritual are inseparable. The physical world, all that we taste, touch, smell, hear, and see — all this sense data — expresses and reveals the spiritual, which is why our God can be experienced on the trout stream; in the sunset, the symphony, drama, and personal relationships; in bread and wine. The sensible, the tangible, the concrete express and reveal the depth of the spiritual. They convey truth, beauty, the very presence of God. This is why Mother Julian of Norwich while contemplating a hazelnut glimpsed the very presence of God who brought that hazelnut into existence and continually sustained it. This is why, when God wanted to communicate God's self to us, God became flesh; God became concrete, tangible, physical; God became incarnate, sacramental. God was born at a particular time in a particular place in a particular way. Because of our sacramental theology we do not separate experience into sacred and secular; we do not separate temporal and eternal, spiritual and material, church and world, Sunday and the rest of the week. They are inseparable. One expresses, reveals the other.

Now let me apply our sacramental theology to what is pressing small congregations in Northern Michigan to reexamine, restructure, re-vision our life, ministry, and mission.

Clericalism and Anticlericalism

We have had a conventional paradigm right in the heart of our church which served us well and I honor that, but which over time has separated us and fragmented our sacramental life and theology. We have evolved in our Episcopal Church in the United States a separation of ministry in the church and ministry in the world. We have enshrined this separation in our national canons where clergy are responsible for spiritual things and laity are responsible for temporal things. That, I believe, is bad sacramental theology. As this separation has evolved we have sown the seeds of clericalism and anticlericalism. We have evolved a subtle and not-so-subtle separation that is often adversarial — a separation that has often isolated, overburdened, and even broken clergy. This separation has often undervalued the laity, considering their efforts as less competent, less valued, less significant, second class, even second-rate, as though anything is or could be second-rate in Christianity. In Northern Michigan we try not to use the "L" word. Lay ministry or ministry of the laity inevitably means something apologetic, inferior, with low self-esteem. We prefer to speak of "adult Christian responsibility," which is what we expect from each and every one of us as baptized sisters and brothers in the family of Christ. In this separation we have thought in our conventional paradigm that clergy have responsibility in the church and laity have responsibility in the world. In the church we came to believe that the ordained could do some things that others in the church could not do. We became territorialized. Let me try to explain.

How We Minimalized Our Historic Orders

We were shaping our new Prayer Book in the 1970s and, as a parish priest in the Diocese of Chicago, I was asked to be on a national subcommittee for initiatory or baptismal rites. I was flattered and then realized it was late in the process and they wanted to add both a token parish priest and a token woman. The meetings were always in Chicago and so would add little if any expense. I was more an observer than a participant. Now I understand what I experienced on that committee. Baptism was to be a full, complete, unequivocal initiation into the life and body of Christ, which meant that consignation, with or without chrism, was placed or replaced into baptism. "You are sealed by the Holy Spirit in baptism and marked as Christ's own forever." From this change there were two clear and obvious consequences. First, anyone baptized was immediately to receive communion, be fed at the family table. The second consequence was that infants were at a later date to make an adult affirmation of their baptismal commitment; in these preliminary documents, that later event was to be called "reaffirmation," dropping the term "confirmation." However, in the conventional model or paradigm, some bishops, several of whom were suffragan bishops, saw their world as shrinking. Their territory was invaded. They were anxious. If confirmation were not central and essential, they felt their reason for being was being taken away. This feeling was so strong that the term "confirmation" was reintroduced. This conventional view of apostolic order was, in my terms, a minimalizing description of the episcopate, what a bishop is. Later in this article I detail our experience in Northern Michigan, which has transformed my understanding of apostolic ministry, my understanding of the episcopate. Embedded in our new Prayer Book is a recovery of the solemnity of baptism, our sacramental theology, and a maximizing view of the episcopate.

Let me turn attention to priestly ministry. In the 1960s and 1970s, as we pursued liturgical renewal and increased participation, priests in the conventional model or paradigm saw their world, my world, as shrinking, under attack, being nibbled away. Some of us were and are anxious. First, other adults read Scripture and led the prayers of the congregation. Then deacons took away our reading of the gospel and dismissed the faithful. Yet we priests held on to the ABCs. Only we priests could absolve, bless, or consecrate, which was a minimalizing and collapsing description of the priesthood. Then we realized we were being nibbled away even from that bottom line. Absolution, forgiving and asking for forgiveness, is not the territory of the priest. This priestly ministry of reconciliation is Christ's ministry for our broken world, our broken society, and our broken lives which he shares with all and each of us through the mystery and power of baptism. "When you fall into sin, will you repent and return to the Lord?" This is our baptismal cry and call to reconciliation, to forgive and seek forgiveness, which was being taken away from us as priests; our world was smaller. In this time of Prayer Book revision, liturgists and New Testament scholars told us that priests do not bless. We offer thankfully to God and God blesses. That is the meaning of Eucharist. To live thankfully is to be blessed and to bless. These same liturgists reassured us that a priest does not consecrate. God consecrates. A priest is ordered by the community to preside at table, and the community gathered is a community of celebration, celebrating the resurrection, our liberation, and redemption. A territorial and minimalizing view of priestly ministry was being nibbled away until the only distinction was the place where a priest stands at the family table. The territory of the priest was being nibbled away, so we came up with terms like "enabler," "catalyst," "facilitator" — all terms where one is present but not a participant, not a member of the community, the family. Some of us had already been cautioned that we would never have friends in our congregation of sisters and brothers. This I believe was a minimalizing and destructive and isolating picture of what priestly ministry had come to mean. I am a product of The General Theological Seminary, the dioceses of Western Michigan, Northern Indiana, and Chicago, including St. Luke's, Evanston. My identity for decades has not been in my baptism, but in my ordination. This revelation will be a surprise to few. In ordination I received a new name (father, pastor, bishop), and a new garment (clericals), and an enormous, impressive certificate. It was not uncommon at an ordination for all of the clergy to wait after the service for others to go to the reception and then we would have a new picture taken with the newly ordained. Being clergy gave us our family identity. Now for the last fourteen years with sisters and brothers in Northern Michigan I have rediscovered that my identity is in my baptism and in my relationships. But this change of paradigms has been dislocating, disorienting, and even anxiety producing. I am developing a list of qualities that originated in baptism and now over time have been squeezed out of baptism and laid on ordination.

Let me now look at the third historic order of ministry, the diaconate. Again, in the '60s and '70s, as we pursued liturgical renewal and increased participation, deacons in our conventional model or paradigm twenty-five years ago saw their world as shrinking, nibbled away. Many were anxious. Now any adult could read Scripture in public, any adult could lead our prayers; next, adults could even administer the chalice and take communion to the sick and homebound. Diaconal territory had collapsed, so that the only difference was wearing a stole over one's baptismal alb and reading the gospel unless it was Morning Prayer. This was in my terms a minimalizing description or paradigm of the diaconate.

While in this diocese, my perspective on our church has been radically changed. The renewal experienced could be expressed in contemporary jargon as a change in paradigm, a paradigm shift.

Why Is It So Difficult to See and Know?

Let me recall what a paradigm is and then describe how our paradigm shift is transforming the Diocese of Northern Michigan. A paradigm is how we receive information, shape information, and understand information and experience. We live with various paradigms. Paradigms are very helpful and valuable. They allow us to receive massive amounts of information, shape information, and interpret our experience. Information that fits our paradigm comes easily and quickly, even uncritically to our understanding. However, new information, new or innovative data has a very difficult time getting through to our brain. Information that does not fit our understanding or paradigm we try to reinterpret, rearrange to fit our paradigm. Information outside our paradigm has trouble getting through; as someone has suggested, "we often do not quite get it." Let me give you the example that revealed to me what a paradigm and a paradigm shift are. This example is one that was shocking to me when I first encountered it some fifteen years ago. You have perhaps heard this. If so, remember back to your reaction upon first hearing it. A father was taking his son to a Little League game. On the way there was a tragic auto accident. The father was killed instantly and the son seriously injured. The paramedics took the boy to the emergency room of the nearest hospital. There it was determined that the child would require immediate and delicate brain surgery.

The call went out for the most experienced, respected brain surgeon in the region. This renowned brain surgeon arrived in the emergency room, looked at the child, and said, "My God, I can't operate, he is my son."

When I first heard this, I thought it was a riddle. Was there a divorce, a second marriage, an adoption? Was this brain surgeon a foster parent? I know given the recovery of the catechumenate, this was the boy's godparent. I tried to reconstruct the data to fit my paradigm; it never occurred to me that this respected brain surgeon was the child's mother. Each child has two natural parents. One is dead; guess who is left? The answer is so clear and yet so invisible.

My paradigm did not include women as brain surgeons. So I tried to reconstruct the data to fit my paradigm. Even feminists can be hooked by this example because all of us have been shaped by our culture to assume things about men and women and what is appropriate or inappropriate for each. This is why those who think too quickly can be very dangerous when they think they understand what is happening through the recovery of the solemnity of baptism. They may well be distorting the testimony to fit an older, conventional paradigm.

What Is Being Made New by Not Being Raised Up?

With this example of a paradigm and a paradigm shift I want to examine some puzzle pieces and then seek to create a picture of where we believe the Spirit is drawing us. For us in Northern Michigan the diaconate broke open our understanding. We had not had deacons in this diocese for the first ninety-five years of our history. So in reexamining and recovering the diaconate we had a fresh, new window offering an unexpected insight. We had no deacons, but clearly we had and were experiencing serious and significant servant ministry among us. If we were to call and order deacons, it was not to have them take from us what we were already participating in and experiencing. We were not about to territorialize what had not been territorialized, namely the diaconal ministry of serving and being served. Because we had not experienced deacons we were not encumbered by conventional expectations. The diaconate became a fresh, clean, clear window through which we could see that ordained, ordered ministry is not territorial. Ordered ministry is not defined by what a deacon can do that we have not been doing for ninety-five years. The diaconate revealed to us that this order was called not to do our servant ministry for us, but to reveal to us a dimension of the depth of the meaning of baptism. "Will you seek and serve Christ in all persons?" Combine this insight with our sacramental theology and we now see that ordination to the diaconate does not separate a deacon, does not raise up a deacon, does not set apart a deacon into his or her special territory. The ordering of a deacon does not separate her or him from the community of sisters and brothers. On the contrary, ordination orders every deacon to remind us, to reveal to us, encourage us, affirm us in that serving ministry that is already deeply embedded in our lives, hallowing our homes, workplaces, neighborhoods, community, and church, but rarely recognized, affirmed, and respected. Where are we served and where do we serve most? At home where we are regularly fed, where we clothe and shelter families. At the workplace among fellow employees. What about public servants, military service, service centers, and volunteer organizations? Sacramentally we see diaconal ministry, servant ministry, expanding, exploding out into daily life at all times and in all places.

We see the diaconate as a dramatic viewpoint into the depth of the mystery of the meaning of our baptism. You and I have had a deep and rich diaconal ministry of servanthood. Now, sacramentally the deacon expands our awareness and understanding of diaconal ministry into a daily ministry that touches our lives at all times and in all places. In Northern Michigan we intend to encourage every congregation of any size to call two or more deacons to help us see the deep and significant servant ministry we share every day. We order deacons to point out peace and justice issues, needs that we are overlooking and for whatever reasons issues and needs that are invisible to our paradigms.

If we as adult baptized Christians are reminded by deacons of our servant ministry in Christ, what about priests? Sacramentally we are about making the connections between baptism and life at home. We are about making the connections between baptism and life at work. We are about making the connections between baptism and life among neighbors and as citizens of our various communities. Priests do not have a territory where only they can absolve, bless, and consecrate. Priests are not raised up or set apart or separated from the community. Separation and isolation are and have been corrosive and destructive to priests and their families. Separation, isolation, and solitary confinement are how we punish one another. Looking at priesthood through the insight of the diaconate, we see that priests likewise reveal to us the depth of the mystery of the meaning of baptism. Rooted in our sacramental theology, priests remind us that we are a community of reconciliation, a community of sisters and brothers committed to breaking down the artificial barriers that separate and segregate and isolate and dehumanize. As Paul was inspired to write: "So if anyone is in Christ, there is a new creation, everything old has passed away; see, so everything has become new. All this is from God who reconciled us to himself through Christ and has given us the ministry of reconciliation. That is, in Christ God was reconciling the world to himself, entrusting the message of reconciliation to us" (2 Cor. 5:17–19). Priests help us see that reconciling with our spouse or asking forgiveness for being sarcastic to a child is our priestly ministry of reconciliation, our baptismal ministry. Priests help us see hurt and isolation and segregation and say, "I am sorry, forgive me." Priests help us see that judges, probation officers, schoolteachers and labor mediators have a ministry of reconciliation. Priests gather us around our Lord's Table so that the Jesus who died to reconcile us with God can nourish and ennoble us. Priests help us see that accepting our own disappointing self is a priestly act of reconciliation. The mission of the church is "to restore all people to unity with God and each other in Christ." We see the priesthood as a dramatic viewpoint into the depth of the mystery of the meaning of our baptism. You and I have had a deep and rich priestly ministry of reconciliation, but our priestly ministry in day-to-day life has continued unrecognized, unaffirmed, and unappreciated. We are breaking out of a minimalizing view of priesthood, a territory being nibbled away, and we are seeing a new day break open. Sacramentally the priest now explodes our awareness and understanding of priestly ministry into a daily ministry that touches our lives at all times and in all places.

Now let us examine the episcopate, apostolic ministry, through this same lens. I knew that, as bishop, I shared oversight, apostolic ministry, with the Standing Committee, the Commission on Ministry, with Diocesan Council, vestries, and even Convention. But to see such shared oversight, education, and witness as reaching out sacramentally into daily life for the baptized, that is an emerging revelation first suggested through the diaconate. Think of apostolic ministry, oversight reaching into our homes, workplace, and neighborhood, sacramentally touching us, the adult baptized, at all times and in all places; oversight of our environment, an oversight so often neglected; oversight of our community life through mayors and city councils; oversight of education through school boards and administrators. For me the breakthrough came when I recognized the awesome, overwhelming, and humbling oversight, not of a diocese, but with my wife, Brenda, the shared oversight of parenting: apostolic ministry unrecognized, unaffirmed, unappreciated. Sacramentally the order of a bishop now explodes our awareness and understanding of apostolic ministry into a daily ministry that touches our lives at all times and in all places. Let me tell you how this integration of ordination and baptism is shaping and renewing the sisters and brothers in All Saints Church in Newberry.

A Small Church Being Raised Up

On January 30, 1994, Super Bowl Sunday, at 2:30 that afternoon, against all conventional wisdom and common sense, a liturgy was scheduled that included commissioning of a Ministry Support Team, ordinations, and baptismal reaffirmations. Newberry is a congregation with an average attendance of 30 on a Sunday in a space that, if crowded, can seat 60. On Super Bowl Sunday 120 were gathered from the ecumenical community and neighboring Episcopal congregations, with closed-circuit video cabled into the parish hall. The support team commissioned that day numbered 13, a third of the congregation. Of these 13 who had prepared together for several years, three were locally ordained priests and one a locally ordained deacon. This congregation can now gather at any time on any day and have a full, lavish, nourishing sacramental life and spirituality. In contrast to the past, they do not have to await some supply person coming to them from somewhere for them to gather, wrestle with Scripture, offer prayer, and break bread. The members of All Saints remember twenty years ago when they were demoted from a parish to a mission because the local economy had collapsed. They saw themselves as failing, disappointing to themselves and disappointing to the diocese. Today they share 40 percent of their income with other congregations in their region for seminary-trained support, stand tall, and have this support team available at no cost to their budget. Today their sense of confidence and competence and commitment and excitement is life changing. The Ministry Support Team of 13 adults pursued their study and formation collegially, rotating leadership and responsibilities. Throughout the process a seminary-trained consultant companioned them. This team provides support for the daily baptismal ministry of the members of the congregation, but they do not minister to the congregation. This team is not intended to do on the cheap what we previously paid poorly for. That would be reconstituting the old paradigm with poorly prepared volunteers. The locally ordained are not in charge nor is the team. The oversight of the congregation falls to the vestry, which has the support of seminary-trained missioners. Where do the members of All Saints turn for seminary-trained, professional background, seasoning, and support? They have three seminary-trained missioners who are available at any time for encouragement, information, background, companionship, and assistance. All Saints is a congregation of adult baptized Christians, and they expect serious, professional competence from their missioners as they seek to make the connections between baptismal vows and daily life at home and work, and within their neighborhoods. All Saints Church in Newberry is an example of what has become a diocesan strategy shaped and being shaped by the Standing Committee, the Commission on Ministry, Diocesan Council, our annual convention, and myself as bishop.

Currently, about a dozen congregations have teams supporting the daily ministry of all the baptized. All members participate in the same formation process, which lasts two or more years and continues month-by-month following their commissioning and ordinations. Our intent is for two or more deacons and priests to be present on each team to avoid the serious danger of thinking a priest is to be in charge. No person, not even the missioner, is in charge. The leadership of the congregation is the elected vestry, and they pursue a circular leadership, as does the Ministry Support Team. Seminary-trained missioners participate in the life of each congregation as companions making available essential skills and experience, supporting the continuing self-study of each congregation. All preparation is pursued locally with periodic regional and diocesan workshops and seminars. Congregations share 40 percent of their income within their region, which supports the seminary-trained competence that is vital to our future and very demanding. For this serious seminary preparation we seek to be a responsible, if not an exemplary, employer. The seminary-trained missioners find their job description very much in the character of apostolic ministry. Theirs is primarily a responsibility of oversight, study, and witness. They are intended to work collegially with each other. Missioners are responsible to local congregations, to regional councils, and to the diocese. Never is one on her or his own. We intend that each congregation experience at least two supporting missioners so that we model the same collegiality we intend to be pursued locally. We hope that the days of isolation, separation, and loneliness are over. Underneath the formation process for a Ministry Support Team is our intent to create a catechumenal preparation for the baptized and those seeking to reaffirm their baptism, which parallels this formation process. Thirty-two members of this diocese have at differing times attended a six-day national conference at which one experiences an intense environment simulating what might be expanded into a one- to two-year catechumenate. The intent of both the catechumenal and support team formation is to reach deeper and deeper into the membership of each congregation until all members have had the opportunity to experience such serious study, reflection, and formation.

Brought Closer to Perfection through Liberation and Reconciliation

Everyone is experiencing a liberation — liberation for congregations that were labeled as failing and unable to experience a full sacramental worship, and spirituality and liberation for the seminary-trained who have exciting responsibilities for which they trained, but for which they, as missioners, no longer have the crushing responsibility of carrying most of the care alone. At every ordination the ordinand is rubrically directed to be seated in the congregation vested only in an alb, "without tippet or other vesture distinctive of ecclesiastical or academic rank or office." I knew that, but I realized that to be in an alb already separated the ordinand from the community of sisters and brothers. Then several years ago it was pointed out to me what I already knew, but had not connected, that the alb is one's baptismal garment. So, if everyone in a congregation were present in his or her baptismal alb, then any ordinand would not be separated from the family, from us, but would by that very alb be identified with us. Making the connections between baptism and ordination — between baptism, ordination, and daily life — will be liberating and reconciling and life giving for all, clergy and laity alike. To take baptism seriously and to see ordained ministry as revealing the meaning of baptismal living, to uncover and recover this paradigm, is life changing for everyone. Clergy may have to struggle with an identity crisis as I am, but be reassured, the adult baptized (the laity) will remember when all that was expected of them was that they congregate around the minister, tithe, and appear respectful. God is taking us into a future where giving 10 percent of whatever would be a piece of cake. God is seeking all that we have and all that we are. And that commitment is what we have truly always sought and yearned for.

God of unchangeable power and eternal light: Look favorably on Your whole Church, that wonderful and sacred mystery; by the effectual working of your providence, carry out in tranquility the plan of salvation; let the whole world see and know that things which were cast down are being raised up, and things which had grown old are being made new, and that all things are being brought to their perfection by him through whom all things were made, your Son Jesus Christ our Lord; who lives and reigns with you, in the unity of the Holy Spirit, one God for ever and ever. Amen.[2]

Notes

1. *Faith in the Countryside: A Report Presented to the Archbishops of Canterbury and York* (Stoneleigh Park, Warwickshire: ACORA, 1990), 146.

2. Bishop Thomas Ray has retired since writing this essay. Mutual Ministry in the Diocese of Northern Michigan continues to grow under the leadership of Bishop Jim Kelsey.

Ten

Re-visioning Ministry Leadership

Beyond Adapting Congregational and Clerical Models

B. EDMON MARTIN and LANCE R. BARKER

What configuration of ecclesial and educational models needs to emerge in the next decades to stimulate faithful and effective ministry? As a starting point, we propose the recovery and enrichment of the notion of baptismal ministry, a theme that deeply undergirds the Reformation convictions about the priesthood of all believers and the nature and ministry of the church. Can we use this time of challenge as an opportunity to more fully and faithfully incorporate the gifts of all in the life, ministry, and theological education of the churches?

The Faith Communities Today Project of the Hartford Institute for Religion Research, reporting on the largest survey of congregations ever conducted in the United States, states that "half of the congregations in the United States have fewer than 100 regularly participating adults and just over half are located in small town and rural settings. Indeed, a full quarter of congregations has fewer than 50 regularly participating adults, while less than 10 percent have more than 1000." Yet, when the public images the typical church, "the image that comes to mind is the megachurch or a high-steeple church."

The report goes on to say that congregations with a clear sense of purpose feel vital and alive. Furthermore, that purpose-driven vitality can be measured by the degree to which the church has the financial capabilities within its own life to carry out its mission vision. "Size makes a significant difference," the report concludes, implying that small churches are less likely to have those resources and, consequently, more likely to have their purposes frustrated.[1]

Perhaps this is not news to most of us. We live daily with the struggle of congregations trying to bring their "bottom lines" and their "faith signs" into coherence. What's wrong with this picture? Why is faith capital so dependent on financial capital? Why does smallness make such a difference in the capacity to be the church? Are we so bound to our images of a particular manifestation of the church in the twentieth century that we cannot imagine a church for the twenty-first century?

A recent movement in community development theory, which we think has relevance for our discussion, seeks to understand and respond to towns and neighborhoods through the perspective of the assets residing within those communities. Whereas traditional community development theory has grounded its strategies in analysis of the problems within a community, asset-based theory begins with the assumption each community is alive with possibilities and abilities for addressing its needs. These assets are the potential building blocks of human and social capital — the network of resources that empowers a local community and connects it to the human and social capital of larger communities. Asset-based theorists argue that traditional models of problem analysis create dependent client publics, dependent on the intervention of outside resources.[2]

Let's look at the asset approach to community development for a moment as a way of thinking about the church and its ministry. Have we not cast small churches in the role of dependent client publics? Is it not true that underlying all of our laments about the state of the church rests the assumption that the gifts these churches have indigenous to their own life and context is not enough to be the church? They must have a seminary-educated minister who will provide the resources of sacrament, word, and care. If they are unable to financially afford such a minister, they must depend on some kind of second-class, less-than-enough service to maintain their ministry until they go out of existence.

The word "assets" was originally an adjective meaning "enough." What if we began with the assumption that the gifts of two or three gathered in the name of Christ are enough to be the church? As Janet Silman notes in her discussion of the learning circles at the Dr. Jesse Saulteaux Resource Center: "Aboriginal tradition is testing: a deep attentive listening based on the conviction that everyone has something to offer, an offering from which others can learn." What difference would that make in the way we thought about the church in all of its manifestations? What difference would that make in the way we understood ministry?

How would that transform the way we do theological education and the manner in which we prepare people for ministry?

We suggest that such a perspectival shift — one that views smallness as an asset rather than as a problem — can open up new ways of being church. We believe that to the extent that we can re-vision the church and its ministries in light of the *enough-ness* of two or three gathered in Christ's name, we can be liberated from blinders of a given cultural age and location and freed to be the church in our own time and place. In Loren Mead's words, "Small is enough. . . . It is enough for faithfulness."[3] To be sure, there is a literature that has sought to make the case for smallness. Carl Dudley's *Making the Small Church Effective,* Jackson Carroll's *Small Churches Are Beautiful,* and David Ray's series of books on the small church are examples.[4] But for the most part we don't quite believe it yet. What gets in the way is modernity's conviction that institutional coherence and enlargement are ultimate values. Still, perspectival changes do not occur easily nor rapidly. Most often they happen when we find ourselves on the ropes and have to think outside our boxes in desperation.

Our exposure over the past two years to the experience of others who are trying to think outside of the box has given us a chance to rethink some of the ways that we understand learned ministry and preparation for ministry. Quite frankly, no one has all of the answers. Certainly, we do not. The task in fact is somewhat daunting, like trying to turn a huge ocean liner around while under full steam. But a number of communities are sticking their oars in the water and back paddling courageously. Changing the metaphor, we heard people involved in judicatory theological education programs more than once refer to their vision as "building the plane while we are flying it." Perhaps this volume can be one more oar in the water or strut on a wing as we seek to find beginnings for faithful ways to be about ministry in our time and place.

We seek beginning places. The Episcopal Diocese of Northern Michigan and others in the Total Ministry movement within the Episcopal Church have identified a fundamental starting point — the reclaiming of the gifts of our baptism. The exercise of priesthood grounded in baptism rather than ordination regathers us in Pentecostal community and opens new possibilities for hope and vitality for congregations and for the practices of theological education.

Such a transformation in perspective takes form around three liberative movements:

1. The liberation of congregations from culturally dictated standards of viability.

2. The liberation of ministry from the culture of professionalism.

3. The liberation of theological education from the exclusive hold of academic hegemony.

The Liberation of Congregations from Culturally Dictated Standards of Viability

While mainline churches recognize and even authorize various types of ministry, the ultimate measure of a congregation's viability resides in its ability to employ a seminary-educated ordained clergyperson. While most of us give lip service to the ministries of the whole people of God, those lay ministries in and of themselves are not considered enough to be the church. The *enough-ness* of ministry resides in a de facto conflation of ministry into a singular, duly accredited and authorized professional. Not only does this split of ministry into clergy and lay contradict most of our ecclesiologies, it imposes an economic measure for what is and is not a church.

Nowhere in mainline North American Christianity is our cultural indenture more apparent than in this manner by which a church's life and ministry is determined to be viable. Any congregation unable to support an annual budget of between seventy-five and one hundred thousand dollars is in jeopardy. Churches that fall below that economic standard are forced to make difficult choices about their common life, ministry, and mission. The result is that churches of about one hundred members or less are thrust into dependency roles and survival strategies that drain their resources, their vitality, and their self-esteem. Their own mission and the mission of the whole church suffers, because all of their energies go toward maintaining their existence. They become way stations along the vocational paths of clergy who are either moving toward serving larger parishes with more resources or moving toward a phased retirement. We should not fault clergy, however, most of whom care deeply for these congregations. They too are constrained by a system that imposes an economic measure of success. What often is not seen is the courageous struggle of small churches and their pastors to maintain a religious presence in their communities and the deep resources of faith that sustain them.

Lest we assume that all small churches are long-standing rural congregations now in decline, we quickly remind ourselves that new congregations are also severely constrained by economic measures of viability. Starting a new congregation in a metropolitan area with a traditional twentieth-century ministry organized around a founding pastor can require millions of dollars in capital funds. Such new churches are almost always saddled with huge debts that compromise their life and mission. Often these churches die before they are fully born because they cannot survive the economic stress imposed by cultural standards for being a church. More often they survive seriously impaired by dependency on resources outside themselves.

Furthermore, mainline churches have been notoriously impotent at integrating faith communities with differing traditions for calling out and authorizing ministry. This is particularly apparent in African American and American Indian faith communities within our denominations, but it is increasingly apparent in our inability to organize ministries within immigrant communities. These differing faith communities are mandated by cultural norms for defining authorized ministry to a position of marginalization. Their ministries are considered to be less than enough because they have not met the criteria established by the dominant culture.

Most strategies for dealing with the viability crisis in small churches have been stopgap at best — yoking congregations, merging congregations, supplying itinerant preachers. None of these strategies question the dominant model of ministry in the mainline churches. Indeed much concern is expressed in anxieties about the consequences of churches not having seminary-educated, ordained clergy leadership. Perhaps we should be asking the question, What are the consequences for faith and mission when all of ministry is conflated into a doctrine of no seminary-educated minister, no church? Can we dream of a church where congregations are indeed ministering communities rather than communities gathered around a singularly credentialed clergyperson?

Suppose that small is the right size for a church. Indeed, what if we began with the assumption that the gifts of two or three gathered in the name of Christ is enough to be the church? What if we imagined smallness as the organizing principle for larger churches and envisioned such churches in reality to be gatherings of small congregations in one place? How would dreaming small change the way that we understand the nature of the church's ministries and transform the manner in which we call out, prepare, and authorize people for the ministries of the church?

The narratives included in this volume are stories of such re-visioning. Each story embodies an assumption of the gifts and ministries of all the baptized. Each program is in the process of working out the implications of that assumption within the uniqueness of their own situations and ecclesiologies. The Episcopal Diocese of Northern Michigan is a fitting example because of the clarity of their theological articulation and the consistency of their practice with their theological vision. After our visits within the churches of the diocese we can echo the words of Marianne Arbogast, who writes in the *Witness:*

> I came away convinced that a lens is being ground in Northern Michigan which could throw critical questions — questions about church structure, questions about the very nature of ordained ministry — into new and sharper focus....What is happening...is more than the blossoming of "lay ministry" or the establishment of "team ministry," and certainly far more than the ordination of local priests. What is underway and often overlooked by those outside...is a radical transformation of consciousness about what it means to be church.[5]

Two important theological principles undergird the ministry strategies of the Diocese of Northern Michigan, allowing them to deconstruct preconceptions and habits of church life and think and act creatively. First, they have claimed the biblically sound doctrine that God values and works preferentially through the small and seemingly insignificant, and they have followed through on that belief by affirming small churches as assets rather than problems. Second, they have grounded their theology of ministry in the priesthood of all believers and followed through on the implications of that doctrine in practice that lodges priesthood in baptism, not in ordination. Bishop Jim Kelsey describes their vision in this way: "We have a specific understanding...a mutual ministry of the baptized; *a ministering community rather than a community gathered around a minister.*"

In conversation with a congregation that is engaged in mutual ministry, we asked if someone gave them a million dollars, would they go back to a clergy-centered ministry? The unhesitating response was a resounding "No!" Reasons for their assertion followed. "It has been life-giving." "We have watched people come alive in faith, in their gifts." "We are working together." "It is a collegial partnership."

What Northern Michigan has recognized is that if we take seriously this turning upside down of the North American paradigm for thinking about the church and its ministries, that re-visioning has consequences in practice for the authorization of ministry and the preparation for ministry leadership. If congregations are to be liberated from culturally dictated standards of viability, then ministry must also be liberated from its confinement within narrowed cultural notions.

The Liberation of Ministry from the Culture of Professionalism

The professionalization of the professions is a well-attested phenomenon in late nineteenth- and twentieth-century U.S. cultural history. Only the degree and complexity of that movement is challenged. Burton Bledstein first documented that movement in the 1970s and argued that it represented a path to middle-class power in partnership with the universities.[6] Others argue that it is much more complicated than that. We believe the "culture of professionalism" primarily represents a response and collaboration with modernity. As respondent to and partner of modernity, mainline Christianity struggled to maintain the cultural authority of ministry through the rigor of academic knowledge and the association of ministry with the professions and with the university system of learning. In consequence, *learned* ministry became identified with the outcomes of academia, and ordination was associated with a particular credentialing model and system. The model was that of the professional — be it law, medicine, education, etc. — trained in a university-style system, credentialed with a degree attesting to appropriate learning, and authorized by a board of one's peers.

Indisputably many of the outcomes of the professionalization of the professions have been highly positive — lending standards, expertise, and advancement to the given professional areas. However, the changing social and cultural climate of the United States in the last quarter of a century has done much to undermine the sustainability of professionalism. Rising costs of professional services, a growing gap among economic classes, shifting patterns of authority, and declining rural populations have been principal factors contributing to a depletion of professionalism's ability to serve its constituencies, particularly the middle class. Most fields today are going through a period of challenge and "democratization" resulting in a broadening of what constitutes appropriate and authorized practice. The medical field is a prime example with additions of paramedical fields and more holistic approaches to practice.

For all of these sociocultural reasons, the model of the professional minister is no longer sustainable throughout much of the mainline church. Churches that either cannot afford a seminary-degreed minister or cannot offer the career amenities desired by a professional with a graduate degree are effectively disenfranchised and relegated to second-class citizenship within the larger communities of faith. Furthermore, recent research has suggested that clergy trained in regional seminaries are more related to their peers — other clergy trained in seminaries — while clergy trained within their local or geographic communities tend to relate more closely with their parishioners. The Hartford report cited above indicates that while the style of seminary-educated clergy differs from their nonseminary counterparts, the effect on church life and mission is not significantly different.[7] The problem runs much deeper, however. At its base it is a problem of ecclesiology, having to do with the unfinished work of the Reformation. As Bledstein pointed out, professionalism tends to lodge expertise, and consequently authority, in the university-trained and credentialed practitioner, relegating recipients of that service to client status.[8] The twentieth-century professionalization of ministry has created a clericalism by which the ordained minister becomes the skilled provider of services and church members, at least in matters of faith, become passive consumers of religious goods.

Most of us in the mainline churches recognize and even try to address this problem by strategies of lay education, lay empowerment, and the employment of various management styles to more effectively involve the laity. Nonetheless, even in the best of situations, we are left with a two-tiered model of ministry. We are but trying to pour new wine into old wineskins. We still identify learned ministry with a seminary degree. How do we imagine a learned ministry in which the baptismal gifts of all of the faithful are recognized and authorized within the life of congregations?

Again, we turn to what we discovered in our research and that, quite simply, includes the observation recently made by Robert Kohler of the United Methodist Church. Kohler is the assistant general secretary of the Section on Elders and Local Pastors for the United Methodist Board of Higher Education and Ministry. He oversees the Course of Study Program of that denomination. Kohler's comment is a response to observers who see an increasing clergy shortage in the United Methodist Church. Kohler noted some statistics: in 1990 the United Methodist Church had 1,413 local pastors. In 2000 that number was 2,096. According to Kohler the point of this increase of Course of Study–educated local pastors is that the profile of who is in ministry is changing, and that may mean that we need to rethink how we prepare people for ministry.[9]

How the United Methodist situation works its way out is to be seen. We are not sure that local pastors or commissioned lay pastors or licensed ministers as other denominations define them are the answer, especially if they function like other pastoral models. But what seems real to us is the certainty that grassroots needs create profiles of vocational call and vision that break the molds or change the profiles of what we know about ministry. Such needs also challenge the theological systems to respond with appropriate educational protocols.

The Liberation of Theological Education from the Exclusive Hold of Academic Hegemony

This movement is toward a more holistic vision of theological education. In calling for a broader and more integrated understanding and practice of theological education we do not intend to disparage seminaries. As we have noted earlier, the problem is not in what theological education does and does quite well. The problem resides in the limited scope and focus and the particular cultural lenses through which we construct our models. Here we would suggest that the first item on that agenda begins with a discussion of the intrinsic interdependence of geography and social location with educational method and curriculum.

This discussion about contextual models of theological education is already taking place, but few have seen the connection between these discussions and what is occurring in judicatory-based preparation for ministry. For example, the essays included in *Beyond Clericalism*, edited by Joseph C. Hough and Barbara G. Wheeler, engage James Hopewell's seminal work, *A Congregational Paradigm for Theological Education.*[10] Hopewell proposed a "fundamentally revised theological education curriculum, different both in form and focus, that shifts theological education from a clerical to a congregational paradigm. The program's main objective would be the development of the congregation, not of the student."[11] Hough and Wheeler join those authors critiquing theological curricula that have as a fundamental outcome graduates who primarily are equipped to apply clerical practices within religious communities. John Cobb, in *Reclaiming the Church,* identifies the "professionalization of theology" as a significant contributor to the malaise of the mainline churches. Cobb argues that the mainline churches in the twentieth century turned their theological task over to the university, which transformed them into academic disciplines.[12]

The liberation motif also challenges a sort of closed circle whereby graduate or seminary theological education and denominational ministry authorization occur in tandem. Liberating theological education from captivity cannot be achieved by merely adjusting the means of deploying ordained clergy (yoked and federated congregations), or by creating second-class categories of authorized ministry (licensed and supply ministries), or by exporting academic theology (distance or on-site learning), or as a last resort, by simply leaving struggling congregations to fend for themselves. Neither can we liberate theological education by laying the responsibility, and perhaps the blame, at the doorstep of seminaries and/or denominations. Seminaries do what the denominations and accrediting associations require them to do, prepare graduate-degree candidates for ordination and service in a professionalized model of ministry. Seminaries remain vital resource and research centers. We must note, as well, that denominations are run by accomplished graduates of this professionalized model. The system is in effect a closed circle.

We intentionally apply the term "liberating theological education" to call for a theological education that is nonhierarchical and embracing of the wisdom of the whole church. The creation of such a conversational methodology will require innovation in theological education models resulting from a deep listening to the yearnings of congregations and people seeking to fulfill their vocations in ministry.

A powerful example of this deep listening is the program at the Dr. Jessie Saulteaux Resource Centre near Beausejour, Manitoba, Canada, previously discussed in chapter 1. As Janet Silman notes, prior to the founding of the Centre, most Aboriginal people preparing for ministry in the United Church of Canada attended the Cook School in Arizona. While this educational approach had merit, observers of persons who went through this process noted that when Aboriginal students left the program of study located out of their home context they seemed to be different people, less able to relate to their own communities. Indeed, some students did not return home. The Dr. Jessie Saulteaux Centre developed its program out of these concerns. The resulting model unites social location/geography with pedagogy/curriculum.

A similar approach to theological education finds experimental form in another program of the United Church of Canada, the Community Oriented Study Program that leads to the MDiv degree but includes only one year of seminary campus residency. The rest of one's course of study is in regional learning clusters. Now, the Dr. Jessie Saulteaux Centre and the Community Oriented Study Program may exist out of geographic necessity, but we doubt that. They more likely represent an authentic engagement with the spiritualities of its constituency in an appropriate learning environment. But more to the point, it may be more resourceful for the bodies of believers seeking authorized leadership.

From these examples, from almost every theological context we studied, and from our general experience, we find a hunger within many faith communities of the mainline churches for the tools of theological reflection and leadership.

If grassroots imagery for theological education is appropriate, we surely have a fitting example in the development of the Parish Ministry Associates Program of the Evangelical Lutheran Church in Nebraska. Five congregations in Western Nebraska found themselves with the ability to support one pastor. The churches were small and were in communities of declining populations. There were no ELCA retired pastors or pastors serving other ministries west of Nebraska's geographic midpoint. A group of laypeople heard of the GIFTS Program in North Dakota, a program that prepares parish ministry associates, mostly who assist pastors. This group also heard of a cooperative parish near Cooperstown, North Dakota. Practically on their own, these laypeople drove to visit those locations to see what they were doing. Inspired with new hope for ministry, they returned to Nebraska, where they helped to initiate a study program for parish ministry associates. In spite of some resistance from the synod hierarchy, the local folk pushed their case, and the program was born. One result was a three-member team of a seminary-educated couple and a judicatory-educated and synodically authorized parish associate. The most noted result is the vitality of the congregations we visited. Out of this grassroots movement, the location and resources for theological education expanded, drawing in the participation of two Lutheran seminaries that provide some staffing for part of the PMA curriculum.

Was this seminary participation a Lutheran thing to do? Well, as one of our lay informants noted: "There always is a need for ordained pastors to assure good order in the whole church. The issue is discovering what pastors and laypeople can do together. This model is sort of a return to the model of the eighteenth and nineteenth centuries. [Lutheran] circuit riders would visit churches periodically, but most congregations got along quite well."

What we are calling for is a broadened and inclusive model of theological education and consequent preparation for ministry leadership that unites congregation-based and professional-based paradigms, educating both community and individual. We seek models whereby bodies of believers are empowered, no matter their size; whereby leaders are raised up and prepared for ministry as the intentional expression of one's being baptized into the church of Jesus Christ. We imagine systems of theological education that include ministries of the whole people of God, all of the baptized. We imagine systems of theological education that include the ministries of the whole people of God, all of the baptized.

We seek a theological education not aimed at, but stemming from, the real life of congregations:

- a theological education grounded in the practices of the ministries of local congregations,

- a theological education concerned for the development of ministering communities rather than the development of the individual theological professional,

- a theological education accessible to all who yearn to deepen their faith understanding and discipleship, and

- a theological education in which the whole church is to be freed for service to Christ.

In sum we are advocating a reunion of the bifurcation that exists between what has been called Christian education in the churches and theological education that occurs in graduate theological schools. The former has tended to claim to give the laity some theological capability, but at a level that is preliminary. The latter, theological education, often is offered to prepare experts beyond the lay level and for roles that differentiate theological and ministerial capability and authorization. In our vision, seminaries would be one link in a spectrum of theological education that has its roots in, indeed begins with, the development of congregations and congregational life. Bishop Ray has spoken of understanding their program in Northern Michigan as catechumenal formation. What if we used the lens of catechumenal formation as a metaphor/model for this range of theological education that we are advocating? What role would seminaries play? What kind of partnerships and conversations would be necessitated?

Many who have called for a reshaping of ministry, and consequently a reshaping of ministry preparation, hearken back to the dream statement of Bishop Wesley Frensdorff. Though stated in a variety of forms and contexts, that dream is collected and published in a festschrift entitled *Reshaping Ministry, Essays in Memory of Wesley Frensdorff*. A portion of that dream statement seems a fitting way to conclude our reflections.

> Let us dream of a church
> In which the sacraments, free from captivity by a professional elite,
> Are available in every congregation regardless of size, culture,
>   location or budget.
> In which every congregation is free to call forth from its midst
>   priests and deacons,
> Sure in the knowledge that training and support services are
>   available to back them up.
>
> In which the Word is sacrament too, as dynamically present as
>   bread and wine;
> Members, not dependent on professionals, know what's what
>   and who's who in the Bible, and all sheep share in the
>   shepherding.
>
> Let us dream of a church
> With a radically renewed concept and practice of ministry
> And a primitive understanding of the ordained offices.
>
> Where there is no clerical status and no classes of Christians,
> But all together know themselves to be part of the laos —
> The holy people of God.
>
> A ministering community
> Rather than a community gathered around a minister.
>
> A church
> In which...each congregation is in mission
> And each Christian, gifted for ministry;
>
> Peacemakers and healers
> Abhorring violence in all forms,
> As concerned with societal healing as with individual healing;
> With justice as with freedom,
>
> A community: an open, caring, sharing household of faith where
>   all find embrace, acceptance, and affirmation.[13]

Notes

1. Carl Dudley and David Roozen, "Topical Findings" in *Faith Communities Today* (Hartford, Conn.: Hartford Institute for Religion Research, 2001), www.fact.hartsem.edu/researchfindings.htm.

2. John P. Kretzmann and John L. McKnight, *Building Communities from the Inside Out* (Chicago: ACTA Publications, 1993).

3. Loren Mead, "Judicatory Interventions Can Help Small Churches," in *New Possibilities for Small Churches,* ed. Douglas Walrath (New York: Pilgrim Press, 1983), 87.

4. Carl Dudley, *Making the Small Church Effective* (Nashville: Abingdon, 1978), Jackson Carroll, *Small Churches Are Beautiful* (San Francisco: Harper and Row, 1977), and David Ray, *The Big Small Church Book* (Cleveland: Pilgrim Press, 1992).

5. Marianne Arbogast, "Liberating the Baptized," *Witness* (August–September 1994): 8–10.

6. Burton J. Bledstein, *The Culture of Professionalism* (New York: W. W. Norton, 1996).

7. Dudley and Roozen, "Topical Findings."

8. Bledstein, *The Culture of Professionalism,* 90, 102–4.

9. Robert Kohler, "Statistical Trends in Pastoral Ministry, 1981–2000" (General Board of Higher Education and Ministry, The United Methodist Church, unpublished paper, October 3–7, 2001).

10. Joseph C. Hough and Barbara G. Wheeler, *Beyond Clericalism: The Congregation as a Focus for Theological Education* (Atlanta: Scholars Press, 1988), ix.

11. James Hopewell, "A Congregational Paradigm for Theological Education," in Hough and Wheeler, eds., *Beyond Clericalism,* 4.

12. John B. Cobb Jr., *Reclaiming the Church* (Louisville: Westminster John Knox Press, 1997).

13. Josephine Borgeson et al., *Reshaping Ministry: Essays in Memory of Wesley Frensdorff* (Arvado, Colo.: Jethro Publications, 1990), 2–6.

Contributors

Bert Affleck is Professor Emeritus and served as director of the Course of Study at Perkins School of Theology, Dallas, Texas.

Lance R. Barker is Schilling Professor Emeritus of Church and Economic Life at United Theological Seminary of the Twin Cities, New Brighton, Minnesota.

Carol Bell is a writer and a member of a mutual ministry team in her Episcopal church in St. Ignace, Michigan.

Ed Martin is Professor Emeritus of Historical and Contextual Studies at United Theological Seminary of the Twin Cities, New Brighton, Minnesota.

Isaac McDonald is the pastor of Wesley Grove United Church of Christ in Newport News, Virginia.

Ken McFayden is Director and Professor of Ministry and Leadership Development at Union Theological Seminary and Presbyterian School of Christian Education in Richmond, Virginia.

Glenn Miller is Dean and Waldo Professor of Ecclesiastical History at Bangor Theological Seminary, Bangor, Maine.

Thomas Ray is the retired bishop of the Diocese of Northern Michigan and lives in Marquette, Michigan.

Richard Sales retired as director of the TAP (Theology Among the People) Program of the Southeast Conference of the United Church of Christ. He lives in Birmingham, Alabama.

Janet Silman is a theologian and writer and served as codirector of the Dr. Jessie Saulteaux Resource Centre, Beausejour, Manitoba.

Minka Shura Sprague is parish deacon at St. James Episcopal Church in Jackson, Mississippi. She previously served as professor of New Testament at New York Theological Seminary

John H. Thomas is general minister and president of the United Church of Christ.

Index

Afro-Christians, 60–61
All-Native Circle Conference (ANCC), 20, 23, 32
All Saints Church (Newberry, Mich.), 167–69
Alternatives in Theological Education Project, 138, 139
American Academy of Religion, 132
American Association of Theological Schools. *See* Association of Theological Schools in the United States and Canada
American Missionary Association (Congregational), 60, 61
American theology, golden age of, 129–30
apostolic ministry, 167
Arbogast, Marianne, 176
Arches Grove UCC (Burlington, N.C.), 52
Asbury, Francis, 84–87, 88
Association of Theological Schools in the United States and Canada, 128, 129, 130, 131, 143, 149
attentive listening, 27–28

baptism
connecting with ordination, 169–70
identity lodged in, 163
Baptism, Eucharist, and Ministry, ix n. 1
baptismal ministry, 171
Barton, Roy, 92–93
Bell, Martin, 37, 44, 49, 50
Beyond Clericalism (Hough and Wheeler, eds.), 179

biblical criticism, 123
Biblical Seminary in New York, 100, 102
biblical studies, Saulteaux Centre approach to, 29
bishops
significance of title in early Methodism, 86, 87
threatened by changes in church, 161–62
black churches, development in South, 60–61
black Congregationalists, 60–61
black preaching, 54–55, 65–66
education growth for, 58
storyteller tradition in, 55–59
Boardman, Richard, 85
body of Christ, 106–8
Botswana, ministry crisis in, 67–68
Botswana Theological Training Programme (BTTP), 69–70
Briggs, Charles A., 136 n. 9
Broadus, John A., 146–47
Brown-May seminary survey, 128, 137 n. 16

Carcaño, Minerva, 93
Carroll, Jackson, 10, 173
Chavis, John, 57
Christian Council of Botswana, 67–68
Christian Council of Metropolitan Atlanta, 70
Christian responsibility, 158, 161
church size. *See also* small churches
changing perspectives on, 172–73
related to sense of purpose, 171–72

187